Unleash Your Inner Goddess

Start Living the Life You Deserve

Christine Rizzo

First published by Ultimate World Publishing 2020
Copyright © 2020 Christine Rizzo

ISBN

Paperback - 978-1-922372-64-2
Ebook - 978-1-922372-65-9

Cover design: Ultimate World Publishing
Layout and typesetting: Ultimate World Publishing
Cover photo: Brooke Flecca
Editor: Marinda Wilkinson

Ultimate World Publishing
Diamond Creek,
Victoria Australia 3089
www.writeabook.com.au

Testimonials

"Christine is a true blessing. She is patient and breaks down the processes so easily. She is very knowledgeable and encouraging yet keeps you accountable to keep moving forward. Christine is helping me to see and believe how loved I truly am."
Patty Myers, Director, Building Pathways

"When I first met Christine, I was struggling with feeling overwhelmed. I instantly felt a connection with her. Within a short time, she's helped me to understand how to address years of beliefs that were not serving me, learn to articulate my thoughts and feelings into action, and manifest my dreams into reality. I am so very grateful for her coaching style and the impact she's had on my life."
Kristin Ramirez, VP of Membership Strategies, Girl Scouts of Citrus

"Spending time with Christine Rizzo is a beautiful gift everyone should get to experience. Christine has helped me and so many people in believing in the abundance and fulfillment in my own life. She is passionate in her work and in sharing the way she continues to make her own dreams come to fruition. I have the utmost respect for her as a person, a Life Coach and an Author."

Caro Szabo,
French Parisian Weight Loss Coach

"When I first started working with Christine, I was going through a very difficult time in my life. She taught me how to believe in myself and to start loving myself, which has completely changed my life. I became more confident which helped me attract multiple job opportunities and offers. We talked a lot about gratitude and I am forever grateful to have had the opportunity to work with her."

Lisa Saravo, Licensed Aesthetician

"Christine is a gifted coach, visionary and dear friend. I first met her when we began our Life Coach Certification program and from the first day, she emerged as such a strong, beautiful, heart-driven woman. Her view of the world always impresses me—real, honest and full of generosity. She walks her talk, manifests the life of her dreams and has an incredible knack for helping others do the same without pedantic jargon or bullshit. Her work has a place in shaping an emerging higher consciousness in the world . . . at a time when we need it most."

Lydia Feldman, Sex and Pleasure Coach

"Christine's energy is quite simply radiant and magical. Her approach to living life authentically and unapologetically will hook you and draw you right in like a warm, familiar embrace. This gorgeous woman continues to amaze me with not only the way that she nurtures her own personal growth, her connection to Spirit, and carefree style, but also her affinity to know exactly what you need, when you need it most. Connecting with Christine is one of this life's incredibly precious gifts."

Sunny Rachel Richards, Life Coach

"Christine will be with you every step of the way. She excels at helping you see things you have not, in a different light, and helps you transform you and your goals into reality. I have watched her firsthand do this in her personal and professional life. She changed to a positive mindset and a new way of thinking which has resulted in her current successes."

**Domenique G. Lombardo,
Broker/Owner Realtor**

Dedication

To the Inner Goddess in us all.

Contents

Introduction

I wrote this book during COVID-19 while in quarantine and I completed it in five weeks. While many were freaking out over what was out of our control, I knew what was possible. I wanted to help make a difference in the world, and I knew the Universe was giving me the best opportunity to do exactly that. I took this challenge on knowing that I could get it done. I was so determined, because I know the power that we all have within ourselves—we are all Powerful Badasses. Whatever you set your mind to, you will bring into your life. I have been telling myself for the past year that I was going to write a book, but I didn't know exactly when it was going to happen. I never questioned it; I just had faith in the Universe. I knew that when COVID-19 hit, that was my time. I wanted to help the world recognize what man has known for years. I just wanted to share with everyone what has been happening for centuries.

Man has known how to manifest and manipulate their thoughts so they can bring abundance into their lives forever. Once a secret known only by a few, it has now spread throughout the world. However, there are still many who don't know the power that we all have within us. They are tied to their beliefs, unwilling to part with them.

For those of you that chose this book there was a reason—maybe it was the title, maybe it was the cover, or maybe when you read the back it just totally resonated with you. Whatever the reason is . . . I am so excited that you did. I know in life things don't happen by chance. They happen because they were meant to happen. You were meant to have this book, you are meant to read what you are about to, and I only hope that you use it in your life so you can start living the life you are wanting to live. The life you deserve.

You have the potential to do whatever it is you want to do. Just like I have. You have the power within yourself, and if you want something bad enough, then you need to go after it. Spread those wings of yours and fly. The world is your story, your canvas. You have the power to create whatever you want. So let's see what you've got!!!

WAIT . . . Before you read any further, I just wanted to warn you that this book has a few (well actually more than a few), what some would call "curse words" or "inappropriate words." I call them "sentence enhancers." They are part of my vocabulary, and if that offends you, I can't say I'm sorry. This is who I am. Real, raw, and true to myself.

What Do You Want?

Tell me. . .

What is it that you want in your life that you don't have right now?

Is it Love? Happiness? Money?

Is it wanting to feel good, because most days you feel life is against you? Are you feeling stuck at times and don't know how to get out of the quicksand that is slowly drowning you? Maybe you feel confused and don't know what you want, but you do know that you aren't happy where you are today? Or you're feeling an emptiness and you don't understand why?

Maybe you want a new home, or a new career? Or maybe you would love to travel, write a book or finally figure out why the hell you are here and what your life purpose really is ???

I know what you're going through, because I have been there myself. I was living this life that I couldn't shake and I knew if something didn't change soon, I would fall into some kind of a depression. That's when I decided I needed to do something about it. I knew that I had to . . .

Well, I just knew that I couldn't go on living the life I was living, and I knew deep in my soul things had to go in another direction.

I felt stuck and so empty for many years. I would fill my void with shopping, and by avoiding the truth. I kept myself distracted by building three new homes, moving five times and putting all of my extra time (when not with my girls) into working, instead of dealing with my emotions and how I felt about my life and the marriage I was in at the time. I blamed outside circumstances for why my life was the way it was, I blamed other people and I never took responsibility for my own thoughts and feelings. I would blame people for my actions. "You made me react that way because of what you said." I thought by ignoring what was happening around me, it would eventually all go away. NOPE. It never did. Not until I decided to finally take control of my thoughts around my life and accept why I was so unhappy.

I decided to hire a Life Coach. I dove deep into mind management, self-help books, audiobooks, and working on learning to truly love myself for exactly who I was. I started showing up in the world by being authentic to myself. And I stopped worrying if other people liked me or not. Whether you like me or not . . . I don't care. I'm not here for you to like. I am here for me to like. I learned to not care anymore. Not everyone is going to like us and that is OK. As long as I am true to who I am, that is what matters.

I have learned so much these past few years, and I want to share it all with you. That is why I wrote this book, because I want to help other women learn the tools that I learned, so they can create happiness within themselves, and learn to manifest the shit out of whatever they want in their life. Everyone deserves to live the life they have always dreamed of living.

If you are unhappy, struggling, searching for your purpose in life, and are wanting to start living the life you are meant to live, this is the book for you. And it's Never too late my friends. I can promise you that.

You deserve to chase those dreams of yours. Bring back your happy that has been lost for some time. Find your fabulous again. Learn to *Unleash Your Inner Goddess* (your intuition). She is in there. She is just waiting to spread her wings again. It's time to RELEASE her, to let go of your past, and start RECLAIMING yourself and the life you want to start living.

You are the creator of your life and you have full control of how you want your life to turn out. Read, listen to your Inner Goddess, and learn. Start taking action to create the life that you deserve. Not what others want for you. *What you want!*

You can have whatever you want, you just have to want it bad enough to take that first step. Life is all about dreaming and creating, to get you where you want to be. Because nothing changes if nothing changes . . .

It's time for you to look at the woman in the mirror and be willing to dig deep, so you can get to where you really want to be in life. Do this for you. It's the best gift that you can give yourself.

I will be right there with you, helping you rediscover what has been lost. Your Inner Goddess is in you and I am going to help you find her!!! That my friend is a promise . . . LET'S DO THIS!!!

And in case no one has told you today . . .
I love you.
Xoxo
Chrissy

My Inner Mean Girl Made Me Do It... I Swear

"Ego judges and punishes. Love forgives and heals."

Anonymous

I am here to tell you that it's not your fault that you are fucked up. That would be our parents and their parents and past generations, who we have to thank for that. When we came to this planet as little itty-bitty babies, incapable of doing anything but cry, poop, and sleep, we were just living in the moment as we were meant to be, and our world was perfect exactly how it was. We had no idea that anything was any less perfect than what it was to us at that time.

As we got older, we started listening to the people around us that we trusted, and we believed whatever they told us was true. From the moment we were able to absorb information, our loved ones filled us up with a lifetime of crazy beliefs that they learned from past generations. Many that have nothing to do with who we are or that are necessarily true (you're not smart enough, money is evil, the world is a dangerous place, there is a place called hell and if you don't believe in God you will go there, you will never find a good job if you don't go to college, all other religions are wrong but ours, and so on).

When your parents were raising you, of course they only wanted what was best for you. They loved you, they wanted to keep you safe from the big scary world. They had no idea that these were just beliefs that could actually be questioned let alone not believed, because most of us are just innocently living in an illusion based on someone else's beliefs.

Beliefs are just sentences that are told to us over and over again, and our subconscious mind turns them into our truth through repetition. So, if your father repeatedly told you that you weren't smart enough or pretty enough, your subconscious eventually believed it. Those untrue words of his most likely made you extremely insecure while you were growing up. You may still question your intelligence and if you are attractive at all.

Knowing and understanding that beliefs are just repeated sentences told to us, we can choose to either keep the beliefs we have or we can change them. I mean who the hell knew? Our parents sure didn't or we wouldn't be so messed up with all these fucking crazy beliefs running through our head. That is exactly how the subconscious mind works: by repeating words or sentences over and over until eventually it believes them.

We have both a conscious mind and a subconscious mind. Most of us are only aware of our conscious mind, because that is where we process all of our information. It's where we figure out how to add, subtract, multiply. It's where we worry, judge and criticize other people from. It's also where we love, remember birthdays, and recall that if we don't shave our armpits, we are going to turn into some hippie lovin' bra burnin' chick from the 60s.

Our conscious mind doesn't fully develop until somewhere around our twenties. Which says a lot when it comes to teenagers, and why they react the way they do. Their brains aren't fully developed. They think they're invincible or that they'll never get caught doing the things they shouldn't be doing, because they aren't thinking clearly, they are still in superhero childlike mode. They do crazy things, like stealing a kitten from the local shelter and hiding it in their sweatshirt so they can escape through the front door without anyone noticing. Yup true story, that was me and my childhood friend. We actually got away with it, and we brought the kitten back the exact same way a few days later, once we were told from both our parents that we weren't allowed to keep the adorable, homeless kitten that we "found."

The conscious mind is the part of our brain that keeps us aware of what we are thinking about, stopping only when we sleep. Once we open our eyes, it starts right back up. The subconscious mind is fully developed the minute we come screaming into the world. The subconscious believes everything it is told because it has no filter to know what is true and what isn't. It believes everything as truth if repeated enough. The subconscious runs basically on instincts and feelings.

Think of the subconscious mind as a little kid, because that is pretty much what its age level is. Most of our information that is stored in our subconscious is from our childhood and it doesn't know any better. If our parents told us that the morning of Easter, a life-size bunny comes and hides painted eggs, then leaves a basket filled with candy, we believed them. If our parents fought every day, yelling and screaming mean things to one another, we believed that is what it means to love someone. We didn't know enough to question our parents, we trusted them. I mean why would they ever lie to us???

We had no idea our world was scary, until they told us. We had no idea that you had to work long and hard, or you would never be able to make a lot of money, or that you have to be skinny to be a model, or that if you have sex with more than a few guys you would be labeled as easy (a slut). Girls, if you want to have sex with whoever, however, whenever, wherever, as many times as you want . . . DO IT! Go have fun, just protect yourself please. If men can do it, women can too. Get crazy, have fun wild sex and then be proud the next day that you didn't have to fake the triple orgasm that you had—and if you have never had a triple orgasm, keep practicing my friends, you will get there. A vibrator might do the trick for you (big smiles). And, if you don't have a vibrator, go out and buy one. Your Inner Goddess will love you even more (wink). The problem is that many of these beliefs you were told aren't even true—that is, unless you choose to believe they are.

Who Knew?

Consciously we are aware of what is going on. Subconsciously is a totally different story. We can't understand why we feel incapable about creating more money in our lives, and why our thoughts keep telling us that money is hard to come by and that money doesn't create happiness. With those kind of thoughts in our heads (which is what we have been told our entire lives) there is no way in hell that we are going to let ourselves have an abundant amount of money, because we believe it doesn't create happiness. And we all want to be happy right?

We aren't even aware that these silly beliefs of ours have been holding us back from creating money all our life. We remain stuck and we continuously self-sabotage ourselves with a never-ending cycle. We want to create a life that we would love to be living, but our limiting beliefs keep getting in our way. We have no idea that this is happening, so how can we fix what is broken when we are clueless to why we are the way we are?

Let me explain why this is so hard to grasp onto. Why you haven't been able to get past these crazy limiting beliefs and why you still believe that they are true, even though consciously you know they aren't.

- *Your subconscious mind has been running the show since you were a kid with unfiltered info known as beliefs.*

- *You are totally unaware that these subconscious beliefs are what control your life.*

- *Your conscious mind is still being controlled by all the crazy beliefs that you have been carrying around in your subconscious mind. Even after you know that's really not what you want to believe. WTF ???*

This is exactly why some of us haven't been able to create the life we are wanting. Why we haven't been able to land that perfect job, or why we haven't been able to meet the right partner. We want to, but our subconscious is in the way. It is holding us back. In order to keep growing into the best version of yourself, you need to get in touch with your subconscious mind. You need to try to understand what your limiting beliefs are that are keeping you stuck and held back from where you are wanting to go.

The subconscious is the easiest, most simple and straightforward path to your dreams. The problem is that we keep shutting it down, we constantly get in our own way by consciously worrying, overanalyzing, and overthinking everything. We start creating our own problems from the unknown about our future. We don't like to not know what is going to happen or what the outcome may be. If you are afraid of any uncomfortable emotions, you're never going to do the things you really want to do. We want to be in control of everything in our lives and that is just not possible. We have to learn to trust that the Universe has our back, that God knows what "She" is doing, and that your Inner Goddess will guide you.

So Many Lies

Our limiting beliefs (beliefs that limit our thinking) can be right in front of our faces, or they can be buried deep inside of us. The best part about all of this is that our beliefs are just thoughts. That's right, every single one of them, they are just sentences that we keep believing. You can change your thoughts anytime you want to, and you can choose to think whatever you want. Best fucking news ever!!! Your limiting beliefs are what holds you back from taking action. They are the reason that you don't have the balls to start a new business, to leave the relationship that you have been miserable in for years, to quit your job, or call that really hot guy that gave you his business card the other day in the elevator. Your limiting beliefs are the reason why you procrastinate forever because you just don't believe it's possible, or that you can ever get the job done.

To change your beliefs, you must first recognize that the belief is just a thought, a sentence in your head, and that you are able to change it. (Repeat that last sentence again, you've got this!!!) You have to consciously replace it, by letting go of the original thought and replacing it with a new thought. You have to recognize that the belief that you are wanting to replace is NOT true, and then replace it with an opposite thought of the belief. When you replace it with a brand-new thought, *it will empower and free you from that limited feeling.* You can actually do this with any one of your beliefs. So let's get to work, shall we?

Question any belief that is not created from love. That is how you will know if you need to change your belief: when it isn't coming from love. Our limiting beliefs are just bullshit stories that were fed to us at one point in our lives. You can start telling yourself new stories, stories that you feel good about. Stories that don't limit you. Start telling the story that you want to start living, because the more and more you tell that story, the closer it is to becoming your reality.

How to Let Go of Those Lies in Your Head

What if I told you I have a solution that allows you to say adios to your limiting beliefs? How amazing would this be?

To find out how to clear those limiting beliefs, so you can start creating the life you deserve? You'd be like, "Hell yeah where do I sign up? Let's do this!" Well here it is.

- *Identify the limiting behavior that is holding you back. Are you afraid to take action? Are you procrastinating?*

- *Get curious with your limiting belief. Ask yourself, what thoughts are you believing that keeps you repeating the same behavior?*

- *Question where this belief came from. Where did you pick it up? Have you thought about this since childhood? Did you hear it from your parents? Did you read something that made you believe this? Did something happen in your life that made you start believing this?*

- *Ask yourself what are the benefits of you believing this belief? How has holding on to this belief served you?*

- *Have there been any consequences since you have had this belief? Have these consequences been painful for you? Are you ready to change them?*

- *Ask yourself if there is truth to this belief—or is it just a story that you have been telling yourself? Find as many reasons as you can to prove that this belief isn't true. Dig deep and see what you come up with.*

- *Connect with your Inner Goddess . . . What are you hearing her say about this belief? What are you feeling inside? Is this belief of yours limiting yourself from living your truth? What is the real truth about this?*

Now it's time to choose a new thought, one that makes you feel good, that empowers you. Create that new story and start acting as if you believe your new belief. Your subconscious has absolutely no idea what is real and what isn't, what is true and what you are lying about. Which is exactly why you have been believing all these crazy lies that you have been telling yourself. Your subconscious doesn't know the truth. To your subconscious everything is reality. The story that you start telling yourself will manifest right before your eyes, as long as you start to believe it.

Our Sneaky Inner Mean Girl

FEAR: False Evidence Appearing Real.

Fear is defined as "an unpleasant emotion caused by the belief that someone or something is dangerous, likely to cause pain or a threat."

In our lives today, there is genuinely nothing we really need to fear. I mean what threats do we actually have today? There aren't lions, tigers and bears (Oh my) trying to eat us like years and years ago when the emotion of fear was actually beneficial to our caveman days (unless maybe you are trapped in the wild). Being afraid today by being embarrassed, or by showing up and being vulnerable because you may mess up during a motivational speech in front of thousands of people really isn't anything to fear. I mean seriously . . . what is the worst that can happen? So you mess up and forget what to say, or maybe you are so nervous that you can't even move, or maybe you vomit, so what, who really cares?

It's not the end of the world. You're still alive, aren't you? You didn't die. Listen, the only reason why you are feeling this way is because you are all up in your head with thoughts like, "What if everyone laughs at me?", "What if I freeze and forget what to say?" or "What if I make a fool out of myself?" It's from your thoughts and how you are choosing to think about what you are about to do. Try to get out of your head and start living in the present. When you live in the "now" you can't find one problem, nothing to stress over, and nothing to fear. Fear is all future based. When you are in the present there is only peace. When you focus on fear, it will become your reality.

Unfortunately, fear is a natural part of our human experience. If you learn to embrace it, and let it be a part of your experience, it won't be able to hold you back from your dreams and desires in life. Each fearful belief you hold on to is a choice you are making. Throughout our lives we absorb all this fear from the world around us, and we grow to believe those fears are our reality. Fear is really just a result of a mismanaged mind. We fear things because of our thoughts about what we are fearing. We are choosing to think thoughts that are creating our fear.

All of our emotions come from our thinking. When we fear something, our Inner Mean Girl (Ego) gets in the way. She makes an appearance to show you that She is still in charge. Your Inner Mean Girl cannot survive without fear. She lives off fear and is nothing without it. She is all about protection and self. Love is nowhere in sight when your Inner Mean Girl is involved. When you give into fearful experiences in your life, you block yourself from connecting to your Inner Goddess (Intuition)—which is your connection to seeing reality, to seeing clearly.

Ego is used to refer to the false self or any self that is acting out of fear. We wind up denying our fear in so many ways: for example, the woman that makes excuses for her abusive husband, or the alcoholic that is unwilling to admit their addiction. Your Inner Mean Girl is the part of you that is in control when you do things like sabotage your happiness by using and becoming a drug addict, knowing that those drugs will give you the high that you need at the time instead of thinking about how it may affect yourself and your family.

Your Inner Mean Girl operates according to your limiting false beliefs, this is all the crap that was shoved into your subconscious as a kid that has no truth at all, as well as all the decisions you've made about yourself that are unflattering and far from empowering. She gets validation from outside sources. She is reactive (my circumstances control my life, it's your fault I have to do what I am doing, I am a victim). She is extremely fear based, and so committed to keeping you safely imprisoned within the reality you've created based on your false limiting beliefs known as your comfort zone. She lives in your past, your present and your future (if you let her) and She believes you are separate from everything around you—only thinking of herself and no one else.

Your New BFF

Your Inner Goddess on the other hand is the part of you that operates with your connection to source energy. She gets validation from thoughts like:

- *I love and trust myself*
- *I know what is right for me*
- *This feels good, this feels right*
- *I am loved*
- *I have a purpose*

She is proactive (I am in control of my life, I am going to do what I need to do so I can be the best version of myself). She comes from love, and is committed to creating a reality of limitless potential. Your Inner Goddess lives in your present (never thinking of the past), she believes in miracles and is one with the Universe. She is your voice of love, your internal teacher. The more you choose your Inner Goddess over your Inner Mean Girl, the more you will see love.

We are all responsible for how we feel at every moment. We are in charge of how we want to think, and we are in charge of how we want to feel. But when our Inner Mean Girl takes over, we start to blame other people for how we are feeling, for why we are acting the way we are, and for the results that we have in our life. We blame the world, we blame the president, we blame the government, we blame the stock market, we blame the economy, we blame our mothers and our fathers. We blame our childhood. We blame the weather. We blame other people. We blame everyone for why we feel the way we feel, why we do the things we do and why our life is the way it is. Your Inner Mean Girl will never admit that maybe it has to do with the person that you really are. She will never take accountability for her actions. She just loves to sit back and blame everyone and everything else.

When your Inner Goddess and love come in, you are able to let your Inner Mean Girl loose. You learn to take full responsibility for every single thing you feel, no matter what someone else says or does or doesn't do. You take control of your mind and your feelings. When you choose to feel a certain way, you don't blame someone else for making you feel that way. You know it is from how you are choosing to think, because sometimes we want to feel disappointed, and that's OK. Love doesn't blame. Love accepts everything for what is.

Start letting go of those limiting beliefs of yours. You don't have to believe what you don't want to. You are in control of what you want to believe. Stop letting your Inner Mean Girl make all your decisions for you. Start trusting your Inner Goddess and start letting her run the show.

"A Course in Miracles" teaches that projection is perception, therefore, whatever fear-based beliefs you've been projecting onto your internal movie screen have become the film that is your life. It's time to become conscious of what you've been projecting so that you can begin to rewrite your script.

Love the one you're with

Repeat after me:

I love myself enough to let go of my limiting beliefs.

You Are One Powerful Bitch

> "Change the way you think, and the things you think about will change."
>
> **Christine Rizzo**

That's right, you read that correctly. You are one Powerful Bitch. You are the creator of your dreams, you are the creator of your life, and you can have whatever it is you want in this life of yours. You just have to learn how to create. So yeah . . . I would say, that's pretty damn powerful!

If anyone has ever told you that you couldn't—they were wrong! YOU CAN!!! You can do anything you set your mind to. You have the power to create whatever you want in your life. Maybe you want to feel happy again, or start a new career. Maybe you want to reinvent yourself (like I did), or start taking dance classes (hip hop, my favorite). Maybe you want to bring love into your life, or start traveling but you have a fear of flying.

If you put your mind to whatever it is you want, you will eventually create that in your life. Whatever you give thought to, you create. That means "all the good" and "all the bad." So please stop telling yourself that you can't, because when you do, that will always become your reality. Plus, your friends are tired of hearing you say that you can't because YOU CAN so start OWNING IT!!!

You are amazing and so damn strong that you can get through anything that is brought your way. Life may not always be easy, but once you come to understand the reasons why we have experienced what we have (to become who we are today) and why some roads that we travel down can be challenging (so we can evolve and grow from those lessons), you can let them go and put them behind you. You are an incredibly strong woman because of the roads you've traveled. You wouldn't be who you are today if it weren't for your past. You have become the person you are because of it. So, start loving yourself for that!

Don't ever regret your past, be thankful for it! But recognize that you CAN let go of those memories that you don't want to be a part of your life anymore. You can stop telling that limiting story and start telling a new story. The story of your future. We all have the power to control our thinking and to let go of the hurt that we may have experienced in our lives. When you learn to manage your thoughts, you won't hurt anymore. You are hurting because of how you are choosing to think, and you are the only one that can control your thoughts. Remember, you are one Powerful Bitch and you have the potential to attract anything you want.

We are Power. We are Energy

We are all made of energy and energy is power. Everything in this world is made of energy. The chair that you sit on, this book that you're reading, the car that you drive, the money in your wallet, the laptop that you type on. The phone in your back pocket, the glass of wine that you drink, the magic bullet that you use (yeah, I would say that's quite a bit of energy). Every single thing in this world is made up of that big powerful stuff. And so is the almighty Universe. We as humans are connected to all of it . . . every single inch. Your Inner Goddess (your intuition), source energy, the Universe, God, our Creator, it really doesn't matter what term you use, because they are all the same, we are all one, which means we are all connected to one another. *We are all made of energy.*

Our thoughts are energy and they get transmitted onto a frequency level. The frequency level determines what you wind up attracting into your life. There are high frequency levels that attract all the good, and there are low frequency levels that attract all the bad. (I will explain this further in an upcoming chapter, "Your Vibes Speak Louder than Your Words.") So, let's start with why you are this dynamic force and where that all comes from. Your power comes from your thoughts. (As a woman, it comes from in between our legs as well. But that's another book.)

We have thousands and thousands of thoughts per day, some that happen to work in our favor, and many, oh so many, that do not. Our thoughts create our outcome, and our thoughts create our life. So, how you choose to think about things will create your results in how your life turns out. This is why it is so important to understand that you have all the power within yourself to create the exact life you want.

When you focus on a certain thought for a long period of time, that is when the manifesting begins. Whether good or bad, it really doesn't matter, because the Universe doesn't know the difference. Your thoughts are attracting whatever it is you are thinking about whether you want them to or not (I didn't make this shit up, it's true). We can't prevent the process, but we can learn to control it. And that is exactly what I am going to help you with. Teaching you how to deliberately create the life you want by learning how to change your thinking. So, let's get started . . .

- *Your thoughts will always control your outcome* (we don't have a choice there; they always have, and they always will)

- *You are in control of your thoughts* (super empowering, as it means you don't have to think bad thoughts if you don't want to)

- *Your thoughts are optional* (amazing news!!! You always have a choice)

- *Your thoughts will always create a feeling that can help move you closer to your goal* (as long as you choose a thought that serves the goal you are wanting to get to)

- *Your thoughts are just sentences that can always be changed* (that's all they are, just itty bitty sentences and you can change them whenever you want to because YOU are in control)

- *Your thoughts become a belief when you keep on thinking them over and over again* (we can blame our parents and grandparents for that one, even though it's not really their fault, they had no idea)

- *A thought is always harmless unless we choose to believe it* (it's better to not believe many of your thoughts, because your Inner Mean Girl is just lying to you most of the time anyway)

You Have Full Control

You have absolutely no control over other people and circumstances, but you have full control over your thinking. I know sometimes it feels like you have no control over your thoughts, but that's not actually true. You have full control. You just need to learn how to manage them. Let me explain how.

First you need to notice and become aware of what you are thinking.

- *Why are you thinking the thoughts that you are?*

- *Do you want to be thinking this thought? Maybe the thought that you are having at that moment is making you upset. Ask yourself the question again.*

- *And is this thought actually true? Ask yourself . . . is this thought true? Is it possible that this thought can be wrong?*

- *90% of our thoughts aren't true. Which seems kinda fucked up I know. They feel so true, but they aren't.*

- *Start to notice that your thoughts are actually optional, and try to notice the feeling that you feel when you are thinking that thought.*

Once you are aware of your thoughts and the feelings that they are creating, you can then decide what you want to think on purpose. (How cool is that?) When we think a thought on purpose that is when you are thinking deliberately, which is going to help you learn to deliberately create. You need to learn to allow other thoughts and feelings to come in. You need to be aware of them. Once you learn to allow your thoughts and feelings by becoming aware of them, you will then be able to choose a different thought.

When you become aware of your thoughts, you can change what your brain is focusing on. (See how powerful we are? Who knew we could change our thoughts?) It's about learning to choose how you want to think and feel in a way that will serve you, so you can be happier. Once you accept that we are in full control of everything we choose to think and feel, you will be able to learn to deliberately create all the things you want into your life.

Your Thoughts Create Your Life

Our thoughts literally create our reality. What we choose to think will create our life. You have been using your thoughts to create your reality your whole entire life. Ever since you were born. I know that sounds insane, it sounded totally screwy to me the first time I heard this as well, but it is the real deal. You don't need to know exactly how you created your reality, just take a look at your life and you will see what you have already manifested. You created that from your thoughts—and you can create the reality that you actually want. You just need to start changing the way you think.

You have the power to create whatever it is you want. If you want to create something new and different in your life, you are going to have to change your thinking. You have to go through a process of change for this to happen. There is no other way.

All the thoughts in your brain and all the subconscious thinking that you have thought since you were little have been creating your real world (freaky, but true). So if your life is a mess, and you are unhappy with who you are, and you have been waiting patiently for prince or princess charming to sweep you off your feet so you can finally move from your one bedroom apartment into the royal kingdom, you need to start making some big time changes in your life and keep reading. If that isn't your exact story but you still aren't fully content in your life, and you would like to see some changes, this book will definitely be really good for you. Or if you are loving who you are and know how to manifest the shit out of everything, because that's how you have been living your life the last ten years, well then hand this book onto someone that you know who needs it, so they can start learning how to deliberately create the life they deserve.

> *"The most common way people give up their power is by thinking they don't have any."*
>
> **Alice Walker**

Learning to Think Deliberately

What does that actually mean, thinking deliberately? It means to think on purpose. Deliberate thoughts are choices. We have to learn to program those kinds of thoughts into our brain and into our lives through repetition. A new thought can be programmed in very little time if you are willing to commit to making a change. Most people aren't aware that this is even possible—we simply think that this is just who we are, psycho bitches that can't control our thoughts. But that isn't true! We are badass women that are in full control.

Some people believe that they are no good because of the shit they have been through in their life, and the things that may have happened to them. You can either choose to let those past experiences define you, or choose to take back your power and not let your past bullshit repeat itself. You can choose to believe you were meant to live an amazing, wonderful life instead. You can choose to live free and be happy. You have a choice, it's all up to you, because you are in the driver's seat, you are the one in control of how you want to live your life. What you choose to focus on in your life, creates your reality.

I know I keep repeating this over and over again, but I have to so your subconscious starts letting go of the limiting beliefs that you have learned and starts taking in the truth of how your life really works. Your thinking creates your emotions which create your actions which then creates all of your results in life.

So, tell me. . .

What is the result you want in your life? What is it that you want to create?

Write that down on a piece of paper or write it in the book. I don't care, it's your book, just write it down somewhere.

What action do you think you would need to take to be able to create that in your life? What is it that you would need to do?

Write that above whatever it is you want to create.

Next tell me what is it that you would feel when you are taking that action? What emotion would you need to feel to create that action?

Put that feeling right above your action.

And last, what would you be thinking if you already had that result? If you were already living the dream that you want to create. What is the thought that you would have?

Put that thought above the feeling.

Now start thinking that thought so you can start living the life you are wanting. Look at your thought, it is creating a certain feeling. Your feeling is creating your action (how you are acting) and your action is giving you a result. You can do this exercise with every result you want in your life.

Don't worry my friends, I know this may sound like a lot of work to do, but you want to live the life that you deserve, don't you? Breathe. It's going to be OK. There's more to learn and I am going to be right here with you.

Most of us don't want to think about how to get what we want. When you stop thinking about whatever it is you want, you then stop the attraction process. What you give thought to, you bring into your life. Again, I am going to be repeating this throughout the book, as repetition is a huge component to creating what you want. We need to repeat it over and over again for the subconscious to believe it as truth, just like when we were little and our beliefs were formed. And that is exactly why affirmations work so well. Try to take notice of the thoughts you are thinking throughout the day. Are they mostly happy, positive thoughts? Or are they angry, negative thoughts? The thoughts that you are mostly thinking whether positive or negative are going to shape your life. If you have mostly negative circumstances happening around you, then you are thinking mostly negative thoughts, and you need to change them.

We were all created to have whatever it is we so desire, and we are all meant to live abundant lives. You can have the life you want; you just have to believe that it's possible. Show yourself how capable you are, I know it is in you, it's in all of us women as we are Strong Powerful Biaches!!!

Christine Rizzo

Love the one you're with

Repeat after me:

I am Powerful, I am Strong, I am Woman.

The Universe Has Your Back

> "All you can possibly need or desire is already yours.
> Call your desires into being by imagining and feeling
> your wish fulfilled."
>
> **Neville Goddard**

One day on my way to work toward the end of the month, I was listening to one of my favorite audiobooks, *Loving What Is* by Byron Katie. I wasn't paying much attention to the speed limit because I was so wrapped up in listening to Katie speak . . . la, la, la, la, la in my own little world. Suddenly, I see this man dressed in a sheriff's uniform practically jump in the middle of the road, signaling with his arms to pull over. Shit, was I getting pulled over??? Yup I was getting pulled over. I first looked around thinking maybe there was another car he was signaling to. NOPE, he was referring to mwahhh. This really wasn't a surprise for me, as I love driving fast, I just didn't realize I was driving that fast on that particular day, I was too in the moment to even notice.

I got pulled over doing 55 mph in a 35-speed zone (see I knew I wasn't driving that fast). I told myself, "It's ok Christine, you're not going to get a ticket, because this man of the law who serves his country is way too kind. So, apologize, smile really big, act like you had no idea that you were driving that fast (which is true). And start crying if you need to." I didn't start crying, but I probably should have.

This gentle giant did write me out a ticket for speeding, but he was also kind enough to give me a break. He gave me $150 break, thank you, thank you, thank you. Instead of the $300 ticket that I should have gotten for speeding 20 mph over the speed limit, he felt bad and gave me a ticket for 5 mph over the limit. (The apology must have worked. My dad always said, "If you ever get pulled over, use your manners and always apologize the minute they come to the window.") Talk about being thankful. I couldn't stop thanking the Universe for the ticket I did wind up getting. I didn't get upset at all, knowing it was actually my fault. I coughed up the fine to the multibillion-dollar highway construction project that needed funding.

That morning, I arrived at work and went about my day. I picked up the mail at the kiosk and noticed two envelopes, one addressed to me from the City of Orlando and the other from The State of NY. The one from The City of Orlando was a notice of a violation for going through a red light a few weeks ago. (I happen to believe they have the yellow lights turn much faster on the traffic signals with cameras than the traffic signals that don't. Just sayin'.) The one from The State of NY was for going through a toll that you were supposed to mail your payment in (which I obviously forgot to do). My $5 toll payment turned into $50 and my going through a red light fine (when it was really yellow, a yellow light means to drive faster to get through the intersection right?) was $158. I am now at a $358 deficit and it's only 10 a.m. What the Fuck???

Oh, I was just shaking my head laughing, because how is this even happening? I knew when I was going through the yellow light, and it immediately turned red as I was driving through, that I was definitely going to get a violation in the mail as I saw the camera flash go off five times. Yup they got my license plate number, can't escape that one. And my theory is, that if you're gonna go through a yellow light and it turns red and you get caught, unfortunately you have to accept the consequence and not bitch about it.

A few hours later I decided to go on my bank app to check my funds, knowing I would have to pay for all my mistakes that morning. I see a debit charge of $200 to Wawa (a 7-11 type store), which I never, ever frequent. You have got to be flipping kidding me??? Is this some kind of joke, am I on the show Punk'd? No, someone actually stole my debit card number and charged $200 at Wawa. It was not a joke!!! What the hell are they buying at Wawa for

$200? Can someone please tell me!?! Is one person just filling everyone's gas tanks up, saying, "Hey everyone gas is on me." Now I was laughing harder than I thought I ever could, (especially over something like this) but I couldn't help it, because I knew exactly why this was happening.

The Universe tests us all. The Universe wants to see how we are going to react when difficult situations come into our life. Are we going to get upset and throw a tantrum? Blaming everybody and everything? Or are we going to accept what happened and take ownership and responsibility for our actions? Life is 50/50, we have good days and we have bad days. If we had rainbow and unicorn days every day, we wouldn't appreciate when life is good. Life is a test and it's our actions and how we react to things throughout our life that help show us if we have grown through our experiences. This I know was definitely a life lesson for me. It made me feel free knowing that the circumstances that happened that day, didn't affect me. I wasn't upset at all, not one bit. I have to say, I actually questioned if I was OK, because I was taking this so calmly.

Instead I chose to dance. A few years ago, hell yeah, I definitely would have had a totally different reaction. I would have been so upset and pissed off and you bet I would have blamed the police officer for being a jerk for giving me a ticket and for trying to make his quota for the month.

When things happen to go wrong during your day, remember that we all have a choice on how to react. By choosing to not get upset over the things that were out of my control, I felt empowered. I was in total control of my thoughts, my feelings and my actions. I cannot tell you how amazing it feels knowing that I AM and will ALWAYS be in control of MY thinking and NO ONE will ever be able to take that from me. Once you understand that you have full control over how you want to think about things, your life will change and start going in the direction you want it to. Don't let silly circumstances control how you want to live. Next time, instead of getting upset, choose to dance.

The Universe Doesn't Make Mistakes

What has happened in your life was meant to happen. The Universe doesn't make mistakes. You can fight that statement but it's easier if you accept it. Because what happened did happen. As Byron Katie says: "Life is simple. Everything happens for you, not to you. Everything happens at exactly the right moment, neither too soon nor too late. You don't have to like it . . . it's just easier if you do." Everything is happening for you so you can create what you want in your life. Circumstances happen for you to learn from, and when the same circumstances keep repeating themselves, it is because we haven't yet learned our lessons from them.

We may find ourselves attracting the same type of relationships and negative circumstances into our lives that don't ever seem to work for us. We keep doing this because we haven't done the work on ourselves. We haven't learned that people are put in our lives so we can work on who we are and we need to stop resisting these lessons so they can finally be learned. Let's move on by learning and growing so we can start creating and attracting the relationships with others that we want to have in our lives.

Take a look at your life right now. No, really look at your life. I'm serious. Stop for a minute and reflect. Are you genuinely positive most days? Happy, giving off an energy that people love to be around? Or are you mostly negative and always complaining about other people? Bitching about how they have hurt you or about things happening in your life and in the world that are out of your control? When you think negatively about things and other people, you are only attracting more and more of those situations and people to you. You are attracting back to you every feeling and emotion whether it is positive or negative. This is how life works, whether you believe that it does or not. Just take a look at your life and you will know. If you have a lot of negative things happening in your life, then maybe it's time to change your thinking, by cleaning up your thoughts on what is happening outside of your control. Start moving forward, so you can start attracting positive circumstances and people into your life. You have the power to attract whatever you want.

Everything we experience in our lives results from what we have given out by our thoughts and our feelings. Life is not happening to you; life is reacting to what you give out. Everything in life is offered to you for you to choose to love. Start asking the Universe for the things that you are wanting to manifest into your life, like the Maserati that just passed by. How you feel when you see your dream car is everything. The Universe brings these things into your life to see how you are going to react. When you look through eyes of love, (by being happy, excited, and psyched that it's on it's way) you are bringing your dream car closer to you. When you are angry and jealous, wondering why you haven't received your car yet, you just stopped the process and threw that car right out the window.

You have to feel love for what you want. Life is bringing everything to you, and by feeling love, you will bring more love to you. When you are truly happy and see through love, and happiness, the Universe works quicker in working toward what you are wanting. When you have negative feelings toward another person, you are manifesting more negative people into your life. That's why it's so important to watch your thoughts so you can witness what you are attracting. The purpose of your life is to love, to love everything around you, and when you do, you will only see love. When you see things that you don't like or love, don't pay attention to them. Don't give much thought to the things that don't bring you joy, or happiness, or you will wind up manifesting more of whatever you don't want into your life.

Your faith in the Universe must be stronger than your fear of not getting what you want.

Trusting the Process

I know you may be wondering and asking yourself, how is this all going to happen? How am I going to attract the things that I want in my life? How is the Universe going to bring what I want to me? How, how, how??? Listen—you will never know how, and honestly the "how" is not your job. Believing is. I don't know how, you don't know how, no one knows how. You have to learn to completely detach yourself from the how and start trusting the process. I learned very quickly that the how is never up to us. It is not our job to worry, or wonder, or question. It's not your responsibility, and it's not your business. That is the Universe's business, not yours. Let go of the outcome, and just let it happen. Not knowing and just watching it all come together is the best part of manifesting. You are able to watch the Universe work its magic which helps you have more faith, and to trust the process every time.

We really are in full control. We just need to ask the Universe for what we want, deliberately think about it every day, and then allow the Universe to put circumstances and people in our lives so we can receive what we are asking for. It's truly fascinating to be able to watch the whole process unfold. Witnessing that you are a Powerful Badass and that you are in full control of manifesting the life you want to live.

Your job is to release yourself from the details and just put your focus on your destination. I like to think of the process of manifesting as a game. Choosing what I want, asking, believing, and then sitting back and allowing it to come into my life. You have moments of, "Holy crap, is this really happening? Holy Shit, I just manifested that!" Remember to detach from the "how", the more you worry and stress over it, the more you are showing the Universe that you don't trust in the process. That negative energy of not trusting will always wind up attracting more of what you are not wanting.

I have been manifesting for years, not even realizing what I was doing. We all manifest, but it's learning to manifest intentionally that will seriously blow your mind. I did this with my husband. He was living in California at the time, and I was living in Florida, we were living bi-coastally for a few years, flying back and forth once a month. He had this great career there, working for a company that he wanted to grow with and one day take over as CEO. I was a co-owner of a boutique here in Florida, while helping raise my two daughters with their father from a different marriage, so I knew there was no possibility of me leaving until both girls graduated from high school. We both planned that we would have to live this way for another five years, until my youngest graduated. Every time my husband would come to Florida and visit, (which was almost every month, we would switch back and forth, one month in Florida the other in California, though he would travel to Florida more since he really loved it here), I would talk to him about how much he loved the plants here, the rain and the humidity (crazy, I know), and we would just go to places that I knew he would fall in love with.

When we weren't with one another, I would envision us living together here in Florida, going to the theatre, walking and riding our bicycles, cooking together in our kitchen, doing his laundry, and enjoying our lives being in one another's company every day. I saw him living here with me, I would dream about it all the time. Not long after, he called me up one day, extremely upset. He told me that he was let go from his job. I couldn't believe it, we were both really shocked, because his boss would rave about his work, I mean he was up for CEO when his boss retired. He was devastated. I knew right then and there, I knew deep in my soul, that the reason he was let go was because he was meant to move to Florida so we could finally be together. There was no other reason.

The Universe moved things around because that is what we both wanted. We hated living so far from one another, but circumstances were keeping us apart. He lost his job in February and moved to Florida in May of the same year. Everything fell into place for him to get here. He packed the house up in two weeks, moved to his parents for a few months so he could list the house. The house sold within a month, friends of ours agreed to watch our dog for a few months until we settled into our new home here in Florida. He sold his truck a few days before his move, and we were able to get rid of some of his artwork that couldn't be brought here. I was able to find us the perfect house that I knew he would love (the home I was renting with the girls was way too small for the four of us, and to top it off my lease was up June 1st. Perfect timing). It was amazing watching it all work out how it was meant to. We couldn't be happier. And he landed an even better position with a company that he has always wanted to work for.

Something that we don't do enough of in this unlimited amazingly abundant Universe of ours is ask for more of what we want. We are so afraid of "Livin' the Dream" thinking that it's just a pipe dream. We are so afraid of asking for more because we think that we must be self-sacrificed and be grateful for having just enough, for just having what we already have, not asking for more. Listen don't get me wrong—it's great and all to be grateful for what we already have, and it is extremely important. But we don't need to just settle either. Life is not about settling. We live in an unlimited Universe that is forever expanding and evolving. We are meant to have desires, we are meant to have wants, wishes, and dreams. That is exactly why we have them, because we are programmed that way. God gave us desires, wants, and dreams on purpose, but She couldn't just hand them over to us, we have to use our minds to attract them.

There is no limit to what we can manifest or create in our lives. Yet we believe from outside sources that everything is limited. We see ourselves living in a world where we think that if we have more, someone else will have less. That is ABSURD!!! That is not how the Universe works, and that kind of thinking will create exactly that for you. Less of what you want. My friends, we are all meant to live abundantly, because we live on a planet where there is plenty to go around and we can literally be, do, and have whatever our Inner Goddess desires. You need to start working with the Universe instead of against it. Most of us think the worst and think in scarcity and if you think that way that is what you will always receive, because the Universe cannot give you anything else but what you believe. Start dreaming big, don't hold back. Go as fucking BIG as you can, let go of the guilt and start manifesting the life you have always wanted.

Love the one you're with

Repeat after me:

The Universe loves me and wants me to live abundantly, and that is exactly what I want for myself as well.

Christinerizzo.com

Stop Lying to Yourself

"What people in the world think of you is really none of your business."

Martha Graham

Are you fucking kidding me???

Those were my exact thoughts when I pulled up the driveway one night and saw the front porch door wide open. I know to some of you this may not sound like a big deal, but to most Floridians that is a NO-NO! No one leaves their door open on a humid night. Do you even understand what that would mean? The "B" word BUGS, BUGS, BUGS, everywhere!!! And hell, NO I wasn't going there!

I couldn't believe it. I mean how many times did I have to tell my husband that he can't keep the doors open in Florida??? (He recently relocated from California and was used to always having the doors and windows open in the house. I seriously don't think that state has bugs, at least nothing compared to Florida. Maybe that's why it's so expensive to live there. Gorgeous weather and BUG free.)

When I walked in the front door, my body felt heated from my emotions, I was not happy. I seriously was out of my mind. (In the past my blood has been siphoned out of my body while I was sleeping, from those blood sucking mosquitos from our doors being open all day.) I have had to tell my husband more than a dozen times that the doors in Florida can't stay open unless it's cool outside (below seventy-five). So, I walked over to the door that was open wide with the porch light as bright as can be (and tons of those vampire bugs flying around) and I slammed the door loud enough that the love of my life knew I was home and maybe a teensy bit upset.

You see it wasn't so much that the door was open, it was that he WASN'T LISTENING to what I wanted. I felt like I wasn't being heard and that he was being extremely selfish for wanting to do what he wanted to do. He wasn't considering my feelings about what I didn't want him doing. Wait, What ??? Did I just say what I think I said? Really Christine? I stepped back and realized why this same action keeps repeating itself. I haven't learned my lesson, I haven't learned to "allow", I haven't fully learned that trying to control what someone else wants to do even if I don't want them to, doesn't work.

First of all, who the hell did I think I was trying to tell another adult what they can or can't do? If my husband ever told me what I should or shouldn't be doing, that wouldn't go over so well, just sayin'. (One of the reasons why I'm no longer married to my first husband.) He can do what he wants to do even if I don't agree with his actions, it's really none of my business. My lesson really wasn't about the door being open at all, it was about letting others be and do what they choose. It was my thoughts about the door being open that made me upset, not the action of what my husband was doing.

I am not one that has ever liked anyone telling me what I can and can't do—so why the hell am I doing this to other people? I will tell you why: it's called EGO. My Inner Mean Girl took over that night and like an entitled brat, She wanted things to be her way. Our Inner Mean Girl thinks in terms of "I don't like it when you do those things, so why are you doing them?" or "Why didn't you ask me or tell me that you were going to do that, when I would have asked you?" or "How could you do this to me? You are only thinking of yourself and not what I want you to do." LOL, are you seeing a pattern here my friends? Our Inner Mean Girl wants to control, She wants other people to behave exactly how you would behave toward them. She thinks ME, ME, ME, or I, I, I, never THEM, THEM, THEM. Never worrying about what makes the other person happy or seeing their actions through love. Where, if I did, I would have had a totally different reaction knowing that my husband loves the outdoors, he loves the humid air, and he likes to keep the doors open sometimes and that is OK, because it makes him happy.

That night was a huge revelation for me. It opened my eyes to my Inner Mean Girl getting in the way again (she's that little brat that doesn't want to play fair, she wants to win all the time). It opened my eyes to understanding why this keeps repeating for me, that I need to be conscious of my thinking and to work harder on allowing others to be and do what they choose to do. It doesn't matter if I agree with their choices or not. It's not about me. It's about them. My husband was just trying to make himself happy and I tried to take that from him.

We are here to learn to create our own happiness. We are here to learn to let everyone be who they are meant to be, and we are here to love no matter what the situation is.

In that moment, I let my emotions fully go through my body, I didn't suppress them. I started to see clearly, and I was able to understand the true meaning of the "door being left wide open." I also realized that every time I bitch about the door being open, I am putting thought to it. And when we give thought to something whether positive or negative, we will attract more of those circumstances to us.

Knowing the teachings behind this message, I was able to smile, see the love and let go of my negative feelings very quickly. Such a big lesson for me . . . learning to allow. I am trying, I really am. I am making shifts as I am able to witness my mistakes. I am proud of myself for seeing and realizing the truth in all of this. Lots of work for us all and so much growth for us to endure.

Don't Do This, Don't Do That

So many people try to tell other people what they should or shouldn't be doing. How they should be acting, or who they should be dating. Who they should be hanging out with or what career they should be choosing. How much money they should be making, or that they shouldn't be drinking as much as they are. Seriously this is so crazy!!!

Tell me this, do you really think they are going to listen to you? Let's be honest here, does your husband, wife, or significant other listen to you when you tell them what to do? NO! You know they don't, and if they do, you know it's only because they are wanting to have sex that day. (Yup you know that's the truth.)

When you tell someone what they shouldn't be doing and they do the opposite of what you are wanting, you will get upset or mad 100% of the time because of your expectations. You want them to do and act exactly how you would, you want them to be just like you. Because that would make you happy. Wouldn't it be amazing if we could have everyone acting exactly how we would want them to? The world would be perfect and we would all be happy as could be, never bitching or complaining because everyone would be perfect just like we are. Yeah sorry, I hate to break it to you people, that ain't ever gonna happen. It's time for a dose of reality. Wake the fuck up and stop trying to control what other people do. 'Cause that shit ain't ever gonna work. Ever! It's like you're on this hamster wheel going around and around, never getting anywhere. Still trying, thinking that it's going to happen one day . . . and twenty years later, you're still riding that wheel. Stop the wheel, change the course of action, get off and accept that telling other people what to do is never going to work in your favor.

You see, people aren't going to listen to you because they don't have to. And to be honest, it's none of your business what they do anyway. You're getting upset because they aren't making you happy. You are the only one that can do that. No one else but you. Stop relying on other people to do that for you. You will keep being let down, I promise you will never win that one. Let go of the control my friends. Do this for yourself. Let things be. You will be much happier. I am not saying what other people do is right or wrong, that's not for me to judge (and none of my business). What I am trying to tell you is that *what other people are doing has nothing to do with you.* You are letting their actions upset you and you will never be able to change what they do. Remember, you are the one getting annoyed, feeling the anger and the pain. They aren't. They could care less. All of your energy is going toward trying to control what you can't. Plus, it's none of your business what someone else chooses to do. It's not your life, so stop getting upset with what is out of your control.

Focus your energy on yourself and taking care of your actions. Focus your energy on love instead of fear. If you were living in a state of love, you would be ok with what other people are doing, because you would be so secure in your own thoughts. Lean toward love—you deserve to feel those feelings. Do this for yourself and for the energy you are putting out into the universe. The energy you give, you will always receive back. Love yourself enough to let go of the things that are beyond your control.

I know this seems so hard to fully accept; I get it. As you know I had a controlling issue myself and I still have to work on myself every day. Yes, life would be rainbows and daisies, and yes so much easier if we were just able to control everyone and have them behaving exactly how we want them to. That is exactly what we are trying to do. We tell people that they aren't behaving appropriately, we tell people they need to do things this way instead of that way all for one reason: so we can feel good about what they are doing. It doesn't have to do with anything else but how we want to feel. We try to get people to act a certain way so we can feel good. Talk about manipulation being disguised (which has to do with our Inner Mean Girl big time).

Listen, people are going to lie, cheat, be rude, get angry, and steal. We can't control that and we will never be able to. It's going to happen whether we want it to or not. It will. What is important here is *how you respond to their behavior.* You are in charge of what you do, you get to decide how you want to think and feel. I'm not telling you that you have to put up with their behavior, I'm telling you that it's not your business how other people behave.

Your only business is your own. Not your mother's, not your husbands, not your significant other's, not your boss', not even your son or your daughters.

Byron Katie states that there are only three kinds of business in the Universe: Yours, someone else's and God's.

Your Only Business is Your Own

When we mentally live out of our own business, by trying to control everyone else's, that is where overwhelm, fear and stress come in. When you think, "You should have apologized to me. You shouldn't be late. I just want you to be happy. You should do it this way instead of that way," you are not in your head, you are in the other person's head. You are in their business. When you are worried about hurricanes, earthquakes, wars, pandemics or when you will die, you are not in your head, you are trying to figure things out, you are living in fear and you are in God's business. If you are mentally in God's business or someone else's business, you are separated from your mind and from your business, which is where you need to be to live your life. You can't possibly live the life you are meant to by worrying and being in businesses other than your own.

We spend so much time worried about what others might think of us, the truth is, their opinion is none of our business. It never has been and it never will be. We have absolutely no control over their thoughts, so why do we worry so much how other people feel about us? People are allowed to think, feel, act, and behave however they want to because they can. Whether we want them to or not, they will. That's just the way life is. We don't have to accept it, but it's easier if we do, because it's not our business, and we can't control if other people are going to like us or not.

People are still going to think however they want to think about us, no matter how much we lie, pretend, or turn ourselves into someone that we are not. When we try so hard to control what people think of us by acting a certain way, we don't get to show up as who we really are. We don't show up as ourselves. We show up as a person that isn't authentic. You can't be the one to decide whether or not someone likes you. It's up to the other person and their preferences and life experiences. It's not personal in any way. Not everyone is going to like us and that is OK.

Take a cute little hybrid malti-poo puppy for example. Some people like hybrid dogs and some people don't like them at all. It's not really about the dog, it's about the person that doesn't like the dog. The breed is the same as it always has been. Adorable, great temperament, affectionate, really good with children, non-shedding, and really small poops, easy to pick up. I love small dogs, and some people don't. They don't like their size, their bark, some people just like big dogs no matter what, and some people don't even like dogs at all (you know those crazy cat people that have fifteen of them living in their house, with fur balls all over. Don't get me wrong, I happen to like cats, maybe not fifteen of them living with me but I like them none the less). You see, the dog has nothing to do with it, it is how other people are choosing to think of the cute adorable malti-poo.

This is exactly how people feel about other people, and whether right or wrong it doesn't matter. It just is. The reason why we want people to like us is because we think we are unlikeable if they don't—but really, their opinion has nothing to do with you and how likeable you are.

Remember, adults are allowed to behave any way they want to. We may not agree with how they are acting, but we cannot control them, we can only control how we want to think about their behavior. What we need to understand and accept is that . . .

People are going to behave however they want to because they can.

What we are responsible for as adults, is how we react toward others and how we can control our thoughts when someone is acting out toward us. When another adult is acting like a child toward us, by yelling, screaming, behaving irrationally or just plain being mean and unkind, we probably want to scream back at them, acting out in the same way, thinking, "How dare they talk to me that way, who do they think they are?"

What some of us don't want to accept is that *we cannot control how others act toward us.* We cannot control how they feel about us. We cannot make them act a different way. We can only control how we want to think and how we will react toward them. We need to stop blaming other people for the choices that *we* make. You always have a choice. Someone else didn't make you do the things you did. You chose to do them, so start taking accountability for your choices and stop playing the victim by blaming other people. You chose to act that way; they did not make you. What made you react that way, were your thoughts and feelings about what they were doing, and then you chose to react. We need to take responsibility for our choices. As emotional adults we learn to be responsible for our choices, our feelings, and our actions.

When we act as emotional children:

- *We give up our control*
- *We feel disempowered*
- *We act irrationally*
- *We hand over our power to someone who doesn't deserve to have it*

Yes, it definitely takes practice learning how to change your thinking, but once you are able to recognize your thoughts, you will be able to change how you feel. You will be in control of who you are and you will feel empowered. *Being in full control of yourself will change your life.*

Let Go of the Pain

When we hold onto anger, we are the only one feeling the pain. The other person isn't, only you are. Let go of what is in your control (your thoughts) and start to enjoy your life. Learn to let go of all the expectations you have for other people. Remember, you will never be able to change them. They are traveling down their path, not yours. Allow others to be who they are meant to be, not who you want them to be. You cannot know what is right for someone else, you can only know what is right for you. No one else. People need to experience things, fail at them and learn to pick themselves back up, so they can grow.

You can show them love and compassion, but please stop trying to fix them for how you want them to be. This is why it's so painful or uncomfortable for you when other people don't do what you expect them to do. Those feelings of being uncomfortable is a signal in your body from your Higher Self/Universe/God trying to tell you that you need to change your thinking because what you are doing isn't helpful. We were created with emotions for that exact reason—to know when we need to change our thoughts. Learn to let go and be at peace, knowing that we are here to learn certain lessons in life. Everyone has their own path to travel. Let them travel down the paths that they are meant to. Believe and have faith that everything is going to work out how it is meant to.

If you learned to just let go and let life happen how it's meant to, what would your life be like? If you were able to just sit back and let life "be", who would you be? Without worrying about the outcome or trying to control how you want things to turn out in certain situations, in other people's lives, or in the world, how would things really be for you? You would be more relaxed. You would feel less stressed and be more at peace with who you are and with the reality of what is. You wouldn't be wasting your time trying to control all the things that are out of your control. You would live a happier and healthier life knowing and believing that you can just be, living in the now, in the moment. Exactly where you are right now. Knowing that you are in the place where you are supposed to be. Because that is where you are—you aren't anywhere else but exactly where you are meant to be at this moment.

If you were meant to be somewhere else, then you would be there, and you're not. You are here.

When you learn to let go, you feel free. You feel content and you are OK with the unknown. Not rushing around, not feeling that you never have enough time, never feeling overwhelmed. *Just simply content.* Living the life you want to live by being in the only "business" you are meant to be in—your own.

So, Where Does True Happiness Come From?

I will get more detailed on true happiness in an upcoming chapter "Love the One You're With" but for now, I want you to know that true happiness comes from within. You are the only one that can make yourself happy and most people don't understand that. They know the answer when you ask them the question, but they don't know how to get there. Their conscious mind knows, but their Inner Mean Girl still believes that other people are supposed to make them happy. This is so far from the truth.

It's time you learned to take responsibility for your own happiness. It's time for you to grow up and start becoming the adult that you say you are. The external world is never going to make you happy. Outside pleasures (money, cars, vacations, new clothes) will only make you happy for a short amount of time. You may feel joy and happiness when you think of those things, but they aren't truly keeping you happy and fulfilled. Once the dopamine wears off, all the shit comes back that has been keeping you from your truth (and that is exactly where overeating, over drinking, overspending, overworking come in, as that dopamine hit will get you high every time you lift the glass of wine to your lips).

We are wanting and expecting everyone and everything to keep us happy, and it's extremely selfish and comes straight from our Inner Mean Girl. When we blame another person for not bringing happiness into our lives, then we are relying on those people to make us feel good all of the time. Why the hell would we want to let someone else have that much control over us? Our Inner Mean Girl wants to stay in victim mode. Wants to blame the world, wants to blame other people, never wanting to grow up and take accountability for her unhappiness. It's easier this way, because then we don't ever have to find out our true faults, how imperfect we really are. Staying in victim mode keeps us a child forever where we can eventually hang with Peter Pan (our Inner Mean Girl) in Neverland and stay unhappy waiting for everyone else to make us happy. But the one and only one who can do that is YOU.

You have to stop blaming your past for why you aren't happy today. When you do, you stay miserable, because you can't change reality, you can't change your past. It happened and it's time to stop living in it. It's time to let it go. You are fighting with the truth, with reality, and you will never win that battle. If you continue to blame your past for why you aren't happy, then you will NEVER be happy because *you can never change your past.*

How To Get Your Happy On

- *Stop blaming others for your unhappiness* (how do you expect them to make you happy, when you don't even know how to do that for yourself?)

- *Start becoming the Badass that you are by doing the work* (it may not be easy at first, but you will fall in love with the new person you become)

- *Start taking accountability for your truth and your own happiness* (it's time to grow up and leave the Peter Pan syndrome behind)

- *Let go of your expectations of others* (expecting others to do what we want just to make ourselves happy is manipulative and will disappoint you every time)

- *Realize that you are the only one that can create your happy* (this is the true secret to your happiness)

- *Love yourself so you can stop lying to yourself* (the lies that you have been telling yourself for years haven't ever worked—it's time to start telling yourself the truth so you can set yourself free)

Relationships are Thoughts

Did you know that the relationships in our lives are just our thoughts about those people? That how we feel about another person comes directly from our thoughts about them?

Let me give you an example . . . Take a really good friend of yours that you absolutely love. You adore everything about her, she's funny, beautiful, outgoing, and to top it off she's a badass in her career. You introduce your girlfriend to me one day. I happen to feel very differently. I don't see what you see in her and why you adore her as much as you do. I'm puzzled as to what you think is so great about her? I thought she was too opinionated, standoffish and a little conceited. Those were just my thoughts about your friend, but that doesn't make her unlovable. Your friend isn't different in any way, she hasn't changed at all. It's just my thoughts and possibly my expectations of your friend that aren't creating the warm fuzzy feelings about her like they do for you. And, I probably need to do some work on myself, considering the reasons why I don't like your friend.

You see, we don't even realize that we have rules for every one of our relationships, and because of that, we have stopped being able to truly experience them. We are so locked into our own expectations of how relationships should be. But, if we learn to drop our expectations and limiting beliefs for others, so many doors will open for us to experience great relationships.

We can start to enjoy the company of others more, by spending quality time with them and loving them unconditionally for exactly who they are. *This my friend, is the secret to all relationships.*

What would happen if you decided to embrace who you are and show up as that beautiful, magnificent amazing woman? Not trying to be someone else so you can be more likeable, just being proud and knowing that this YOU, this is who you were always meant to be, no matter what anyone else thinks? This is who you are and understanding that if the other person doesn't like small hybrid dogs, it's totally fine. It's nothing personal. How would you feel? Who would you be? How would you act? These are the questions you need to ask yourself so you can start living as that person again, so you can set yourself free from those limiting beliefs.

When you put yourself out there, most people don't give a shit, and those that have an opinion of you, will either like you, or they won't. When you learn to love yourself enough, you won't give a fuck either way. That is where you want to be. Understanding that we are not put on this earth to make other people happy, we are here to create our own happiness. When you're okay with other people's opinions and criticisms of you, you will be willing to take more risks than you've ever dreamed of taking. You won't care what someone else thinks of you. By showing up as exactly who you are meant to show up as, you will be confident as fuck. Loving every bit of yourself for who you are. It's time to unleash that Inner Goddess of yours and start owning who you truly are!

Love the one you're with

Repeat after me:

I create my own happiness because no one else can.

Mirror, Mirror, on the Wall, Who is the Most Perfect of Them All?

"If we learn to open our hearts, anyone, including the people who drive us crazy, can be our teachers."

Pema Chodron

Are there people in your life that push your buttons? That annoy the hell out of you? That happen to drive you out of your fucking mind? Yes, relationships are complicated my friends, we all have people in our lives that drive us mad, and we all know someone that we wish we didn't have to be around as often as we are. I mean why does this happen? Why do so many people in our lives drive us crazy? And why the hell are they constantly always around us?

I went through this for so many years. I didn't like many people. Too many things about other people would annoy the crap out of me. Like their attitude, how they were always angry, or how they weren't acting how I felt they should be. How people can be rude and obnoxious. And my all-time favorite, how some people drive too damn slow in the fast lane (well come on, I still feel that way . . . we all know that really is annoying!!!). Ohhh, I could go on and on. I would just blame, blame, blame everyone else for their faults. Never once wanting to see that I had a few of my own. Nope not me. I was practically perfect in my own little world, judging everyone else—but not myself.

I eventually learned that the people who tend to annoy the hell out of us, and spew out dragon fire toward us, happen to be our best teachers. Which unfortunately meant that I had some shit to figure out with who I was. When I first heard all this crazy talk about other people being our mirrors, I was like "What the hell are they talking about?" "How can that possibly be true?" I refused to believe any of this. There was absolutely no way that I could possibly have that many lessons to learn, let alone all those things wrong with me. (I was practically perfect, remember?) The truth is, that the person that succeeds in pushing your buttons is the exact mirror image of your lessons. Once I understood this, I knew I had to start working on myself, because I really didn't like the person I had become.

I know hearing this feels like the door is being slammed in your face (especially now that you may have to start working on yourself). Trust me when I first heard this, I wanted absolutely nothing to do with it. I would fight it every time, trying to make it like the person annoying the hell out of me really wasn't, because I didn't want to have to admit that I was less than perfect. And guess what? More and more people that continued to annoy me started continuously showing up in my life. I couldn't escape them. Everywhere I turned, someone was wanting to control a situation, a person, a conversation that they weren't able to. And then I realized: if I don't work on myself, this isn't going to stop, and I am just going to keep running into these people trying to control everything. Unless I choose to never leave the house again. I just wasn't sure what I needed to work on. I knew I didn't have control issues (Laughing out loud), I considered myself laid back, a go with the flow type of girl. Then my eyes opened to reality. Wait a minute . . . Holy crap, I am one of "those people" trying to control other people myself. (LOL, shaking my head.) OH MY GOD CHRISTINE. You've been judging all of these people and you are just as bad, sometimes even worse!

I just laughed, and laughed, and laughed. And then I cried. I cried like a baby. I couldn't get over how I had such anger toward others, people that I didn't even know. How I was judging them thinking that there were so many things wrong with who they were. Until I finally took full accountability that *I was angry with who I was showing up as.* I was angry with how I was trying to control other people, circumstances, and conversations. I was so upset with myself for blaming other people for being how I perceived them, when really, I didn't really like who I was. I wasn't seeing the good in who they all were. I was just seeing what was obvious to me in what I was seeing in myself. So, I made a commitment to myself. To start working on how I wanted to start showing up in the world, and that is exactly when I hired my first Life Coach and we dove in deep. I knew the person I was at the time wasn't who I truly was, and there was no way in hell that I was going to let the thoughts and feelings I was having define me.

Nope. Can't Possibly Be True

I will never forget the day that my life coach made me aware of how much I feel the need to control other people. During one of our sessions, I was bitching about my husband and his behavior. Not realizing that I was trying to control how he should act, and not seeing that I only wanted him to act a certain way so I could feel good. I wasn't buying what she was putting down. I kept telling her, "No, I don't think you understand what is really going on here. He is hurting himself by doing what he is doing." I then told her. "This really has nothing to do with me at all. No, you really don't understand, I just want to help him, I want him to be OK." She said back to me, "Oh no I understand quite well. Let me ask you this: How do you know that what he is doing is hurting him? Are you his doctor? How could you possibly know what is good for him and what isn't? It sounds like he is happy doing what he is doing."

She went on. "You're the one that isn't happy about it. You're the one that is getting annoyed and judging him.

You are bringing your past experiences into your marriage and you are letting your thoughts about what he is doing affect how you feel. It's not actually about the act of what your husband is doing. It is about how you are choosing to think of it. This is your lesson Christine, this has nothing to do with him, this is about you and about allowing others to be who they are meant to be. He's an adult, just like you are. How does it make you feel when other people tell you what to do? You probably don't like it, and guess what, you are doing exactly that—telling your husband what he should and shouldn't be doing. You need to let go of the control and let him live his experience. Your life is not his. He has his own lessons. You want him to act a certain way and do certain things so you can feel good. This is not at all about him. This is about you."

I had to stop and take it all in. That was a lot to digest and I didn't want to see it that way at all. I was waiting for her to tell me that I was right and yes, he needed to fix his behavior. We sat in silence for a good five minutes. I didn't want to wrap my brain around this. I thought I did all of this work already? What the hell ??? Why is this still happening to me? I knew I needed to dig deeper, I knew I needed to fully let go. She was right. This was ALL about me and had absolutely nothing to do with him.

Most of us have control issues, that we don't see in ourselves, but we see in others. We want other people to act a certain way so we can feel good about how they are behaving, and that is not reality, or how things work.

WE CANNOT CONTROL PEOPLE. Please take that in and reread that last sentence. We want to, but it doesn't work, and it never will. Trying to control someone is like trying to hold a beach ball underwater. It comes shooting up from the pressure of trying to keep the ball held down. Every person has their own path in life, and we cannot possibly know what is right for another person. We think we do because of our experiences from our past, but we don't. You are the only person that knows what is right for you. No one else but you. The same goes for other people. We don't know and we won't ever know what is right or wrong for them. My clients ask me all the time what I think they should do in a situation, I tell them that I couldn't possibly know what they should do, I may know what I would do in that situation, but that doesn't mean that is what they should do. We all have the answer within ourselves. If you ask for an answer, you will find that answer within, from your Inner Goddess. She will always answer you if you ask for her guidance.

It started to all make sense to me, that what we focus on, we will create more of in our life. I was the one attracting all of those people to me. Whatever you put thought to, you will attract in your life, both positive and negative, and that is exactly what I was doing. Attracting the exact same like-minded people into my life as myself. It was annoying at the time and it drove me crazy until I realized that I was the one that created all of this myself. All these people were in my life for me to learn and grow from (I mean who knew?). I am grateful that the Universe put those people in my life so I can learn, grow, and move on to the next. Today, I don't seem to attract many people in my life that like to control things, and if I do, I don't even notice because I don't see that in other people anymore. It may have taken a few years of digging deep, but I got there and I love myself for finally becoming who I have always wanted to be.

Get Me Off This Hamster Wheel

Our lessons in life are meant for us to grow and figure out the issues we have within ourselves. That is exactly why we keep repeating the same stupid mistakes over and over and over again. (Think *Groundhog Day*. I never liked that movie, I now know why.) Like those boys/girls that we kept dating even though they were treating us like crap, or the friends that took advantage of us because we were too afraid to speak up and say NO to anything they asked us to do, thinking they wouldn't be friends with us anymore. We will continue to attract and repeat over and over the same problems and people, until we learn the lessons we are supposed to. We are meant to evolve; we are meant to grow. We are meant to learn and accept people for who they are and to let go of the control. Aren't you tired already from repeating the same fucking mistakes? Now you know why you keep attracting the same situations into your life. Take this in and start learning those lessons so you can stop repeating the same mistakes. It's seriously exhausting. Let's start learning something fun like how to deliberately attract the things you actually want in your life, not the things you don't want anymore.

> *"I'm not offended by all the dumb blonde jokes, because I know I'm not dumb, I also know I'm not blonde."*
>
> **Dolly Parton**

Our reality is a mirror of our thoughts, the people in our lives are included in that mirror. The way we see people is who we really are, because our thoughts create our reality. The same is true for what people say toward us, and about us. Let me give you an example. You probably wouldn't take offense if someone made fun of your purple curly hair when you actually have straight blonde hair. (Not that there's anything wrong with purple curly hair, I love purple hair and I love curls, I curl my hair all the time.) You wouldn't think anything of it because you would know that it's not true. You would actually think there may be something wrong with their eyesight since they have no clue what they are talking about. But if someone maybe teased you about being difficult or that you are extremely opinionated, you may then take offense to that, questioning yourself if they may be right, or if you really are that way? And do other people actually see you that way? But, if you knew it wasn't true, it wouldn't bother you in any way at all. When you get annoyed or upset by someone else's thoughts about you, that is a cue that you my friend need to do some work on yourself.

While anyone you meet at any time can act as a self-reflective mirror, most often it's the people who play important roles in our lives that give us an even better opportunity for growth and to learn more about who we are. Those are the people who really know how to push our buttons (our significant others, our parents, our children, our siblings). Yes, they know exactly how to push them, and they wind up pushing them more often than they should ever be allowed to. But, that is where our lessons come from my friends.

Unfortunately, the things that stand out the most about other people are the things that remind us the most of ourselves—because other people are like mirrors to us. If someone annoys the hell out of you, you're actually projecting onto them what you don't happen to like about yourself. Same goes for if you think someone is amazing, they are reflecting back something that you see in yourself that you like. Your reality is created by what you focus on and your perception of how you choose to see it. This goes for everything in your life including all the things you focus on about all the people in your world. We are attracted to and turned off by many things about other people. The same things we are attracted to and turned off in who we are.

Once we have fully accepted another person for who they are, the other person won't annoy us anymore. If your friends, neighbors, coworkers, clients, or any of your family members like your Aunt Joni, with the annoying way she always talks about herself and never lets anyone else get a word in, happens to bother you, this is because you need to look deeper within yourself and ask . . . What do I need to learn from this person? Am I controlling like that with conversations or maybe I am controlling in other areas of my life? Or maybe I need to be a better listener? These are our teachers that help us grow. You will know that you have made a shift in the right direction once the person stops annoying the hell out of you.

Not everyone needs to work on the same lessons in life and that is exactly why some people who annoy us don't always annoy other people. You may be thinking, "Of course my mother annoys the crap out of everyone, how could she not? I mean have you met her???" The reason they don't is because other people have different lessons to learn than you. What bothers one person won't necessarily bother someone else. It's all about the individual work we need to do within ourselves.

It's You. You and Only You

We aren't here to depend on others to create our happiness. That comes from you. That comes from within. No one else. You are the only one that will ever be able to create your own happiness, because you are the only one that knows how to do that. Not your husband, not your wife, not your significant other, not your children, not even your best friend (well, unless there is a bottle of wine involved). No one will ever be able to know how to make you happy. Come on, half the time, you don't even know how to create your own happiness, so how the fuck do you expect anyone else to know??? Mmmmhmmmm, that's what I thought.

Life is about trying to learn how to create our own happiness. Sure, this shit ain't easy, which is why we expect others to create our happiness for us. We expect others to make us happy. Now that makes me laugh! Learn to make yourself happy, 'cause no one else is going to. Your expectations have been getting in the way and they always will, until you drop that shit and start making yourself happy. Love the one you're with . . . as in "Yourself." It's you, you and only YOU. Life is like a game— it's all about lessons, figuring out what makes us happy and learning to create that for ourselves. We all deserve to have whatever we want in life; we just need to figure out how to create it. The Universe wants us to be happy, the Universe wants us to live abundantly, we just have to learn *how*. And this means having the right mindset to go out, search for it, find it, and *make it happen*.

When you love yourself enough to make those changes in yourself, everyone benefits. You will start attracting the right people and circumstances into your life that are in alignment with who you are. The people that used to bug the crap out of you, won't bother you anymore. You will be a new person on a different frequency level, experiencing different people for exactly who they are and you will be loving life, because life is exactly how you perceive it. As Wayne Dyer says: "Change the way you look at things, and the things you look at change." Brilliant man.

At the end of the day, it's not about them, it's about you loving yourself, believing that you are worthy to be seen for who you really are. It's about learning to let go of your limiting beliefs and working on new beliefs and of what you want to start believing. You can choose to believe whatever you want about who you are. How you decide to think about yourself, is who you will become.

Own Your Shit and Get Curious

When you're with other people, start noticing what triggers you. What about them bothers you? And instead of judging them or bitching about them, look at yourself in the mirror, get curious as to what it is about them that really annoys the hell out of you and then turn it around. You may actually see yourself doing those same exact things to other people but you never stopped to take notice. Get real with who you are, dig deep, ask your Inner Goddess—she will help you start seeing things more clearly.

Who Would You Be If You Weren't This Way?

You would be happy, more at peace and not in other people's business where you don't belong. In order to be happier, you now know that you need to stop trying to control what other people do by insisting that they do things exactly how you would do them. Let go of the control. It hasn't worked for you so far, so what makes you think it ever will? Take notice of your habits and your beliefs and start loving yourself enough to let go, by letting others be where they are meant to be . . . in their business.

Love the Goddess you are. You can do anything! You are amazing. You always have been and you always will be. Start loving yourself and believing in who you are. You are one powerful bitch and you are going to learn to create the life you deserve.

Nothing will ever go away until it has taught us what we need to learn.

Love the one you're with

Repeat after me:

Mirror, mirror, on the wall, I am Love after all.

Christinerizzo.com

Love the One You're With

"If we really love ourselves, everything in our life works."

Louise Hay

Unfuckwithable: (adj.) When you love yourself so much that you are truly at peace and in touch with who you are, and nothing anyone says or does bothers you, and no negativity or drama can ever touch you.

Self-love is the key ingredient for internal power and is essential to living a life of happiness. When we let go of our Inner Mean Girl's false perception of who we are or who we feel we need to be, we can learn to become our true selves, which is that of love. The love that we are talking about here is our Inner Goddess, reminding us that we are great and we are worthy, helping us to let go of all resentment, leading us in the right direction, where we are able to think and act through love. Self-love is no different from the love that you show others. When we put ourselves down, and disrespect who we are, we are putting that out into the world. Our energy level is affected when we self-inflict with negativity. That negative energy spreads like wildfire, just like a virus. The more people who function from a low-level energy, and from fear, the more hate, violence, and war there is in the world.

When you start searching for self-love from external circumstances or through other people, you will never, ever be fulfilled. You will be on an endless search, struggling to find enough approval and love—and it will never be enough, because others can't make us happy. That is when, through love, we try to complete other people so we can feel worthy and good enough, since we aren't giving that to ourselves. Lack of self-love can be extremely destructive. All the negative thoughts that you have about yourself that you are incapable, lazy, a worthless loser are just illusions from your misplaced thoughts.

Listen: it is just as easy to believe that you're amazing, as it is to believe that you suck at everything you do. Why is it that other people see you as this incredible person, but you can't see that at all? If you are wanting to live a happy life, it's time to let go of all the drama so you can start to reconnect with your sense of self-love. Through affirmations, meditation, self-kindness and forgiving, you will be able to rebuild the love that has always been inside of you, the love you were created with. Once that inner shift takes place, you will start shaking those hips of yours, jumping up and down, and feeling like a "Free Bitch Baby" now that you are not bound by those shackles of insecurity anymore.

One day on social media, I posted a post titled "How's Your Vagina" that offended many. (It's a really good read and super funny, you can view it on my Facebook page Christine. rizzodavi or on my Instagram page Christinerizzo444.) For some, the post may have been shocking. Some may have hated it, loved it, or thought I was crazy to post what I did. And that was truly OK. I didn't post it wanting everyone to like it or love it. I posted it because the message in my content was deeper than that. It was about respecting yourself, loving yourself, and taking care of yourself. And it was about being TRUE to MYSELF. I didn't care what some people thought about my post, those were just their thoughts and I wasn't going to let their opinion bother me or stop me from being my authentic self. (Seriously check it out when you have the time. It will definitely raise your frequency level and have you laughing your ass off.)

Not everyone is going to love us or like us, and that is OK. Who cares? So what? That's their problem, not yours. They're the one feeling those feelings not you. Let them if they choose to. And FYI, it's none of your business anyway. We are not here to please everyone, and when we try to, that is when true resentment follows. The truth is that by trying to people please, you are doing it so you can feel good, by trying to get them to like or love you more. This concept doesn't work because you CAN'T and you WON'T be able to make people happy. I know I keep repeating this over and over again, but I need to so that you can start making yourself happy. We can't make other people happy, that is their job, just like your job is learning how to make yourself happy. Remember you are the one feeling upset or mad because they didn't give you the reaction that you were expecting them to. People are going to do things their way, not how you want them to. Just because they aren't conforming to your beliefs doesn't mean that they are wrong. There is no right or wrong, there just is. It may actually be your beliefs that you need to question.

Respect Yourself Enough to Say No

It really is OK to say no. When you're saying no, you're saying it out of love for yourself, by not doing something for someone that you really didn't want to do anyway. When you say yes to something and you really didn't want to do what was asked of you, resentment follows. Then when you want the person to do something and they say no, you get mad because of your expectations. *Stop expecting. Be true to yourself. And start saying NO.*

Stay Authentic to WHO YOU Are!

- *COMMIT to YOURSELF*
- *LOVE YOURSELF*
- *BE TRUE to YOURSELF*

YOU are worth all the LOVE in the world. No words are TRUER than those. YOU are an amazing human being. YOU are worthy, beautiful, 100% lovable and that is the truth!!!

There will NEVER be another YOU, so LOVE every bit of yourself damn it!!!

It's about loving yourself enough, by being true to who YOU are. You are a child of God, of the Universe, of our Creator, and you were created perfectly. Exactly how you were meant to be created. You are perfectly perfect. Every negative thought that you have become attached to about who you are is futile in every way (that you're too fat, you're not pretty enough, you're not good at love or relationships, or that you are still a drug addict, even though you haven't used in fifteen years). They are all useless, they are all lies that you have been telling yourself, every single one of them. Unless your thoughts are from love, they are not true. If they are negative and from fear, that is when you know they aren't true and you need to change them.

You Are Perfectly Perfect

The perfect you isn't something that you need to create, because God has already created it. You are already perfect. The love within you is perfect, and that is what you are made up of. Pure love from the Universe. Your job is to disconnect from your Inner Mean Girl, as she tells you lie after lie after lie about who you really aren't. You need to start trusting your Inner Goddess as she only tells you the truth, which is that of love. Nothing that you have done or will do in this lifetime will ever change who you are and how your creator feels for you. (Not even if you went cow tipping years ago, or if when you were younger you lied to your parents when they asked you if you made your brother Tommy eat a worm because he made fun of the dress you were wearing. Not even if you are someone today, that lies, cheats or steals.)

You are deserving in Her eyes not because of what you have done, but because of what you are. What you do or don't do in your life is not what determines your essential value. Your growth is what determines what you do and don't do. And that is why our Creator is totally accepting of exactly who you are today. The love in one of us is the love in all of us, we are all connected universally, we are all one, and we were all created equally. That's right, my friends, you are one with your mother, your sister, the mailman, the guy picking his nose in the car, the homeless woman, the drug dealer, the woman working her ass off at the strip club so she can put her kids through school, the Uber driver, the drunk guy sitting at the bar every night, and the person in the S&M store buying a flogger to use on their client later tonight. We are all one and we are all love. And by the way, in case you didn't know, you aren't who you think you are and you never have been. You're not the one that didn't graduate from college, you're not the one that isn't smart enough because you got turned down when you applied to Yale. You're not the one that can't hold a job. You're not defined by how much money you have in the bank.

We are who the Universe created us to be, we are all love and we are all one, and the mighty power of the Universe is within us all. You are not your weaknesses, you are not your anger, you are not your insecurities: you are so much more. You are a Powerful Bitch, ready to take on the world and create the life you deserve.

True happiness comes from within. You are the only one that can make yourself happy. No one else can but you. Most people have a hard time understanding that we are the creators of our happiness, that we are the ones that need to love ourselves enough to create the happiness that we are searching for. We try to seek our happiness through other people, but that never seems to work. We want to believe that other people are supposed to make us happy, which is illogical. By taking care of other people's needs when we can't even take care of our own. We don't even know how to make ourselves happy. It's actually pretty comical when you think about it. How about, you take care of your needs, and I will take care of mine and then we will make ourselves happy and just enjoy one another.

Learning to Accept, Not Expect

This is the key to every relationship out there. Friend, coworker, mother-in-law, husband, wife, child, boss, neighbor, stranger in the grocery store. When we expect someone else to make us happy, we wind up waiting forever because that ship has sailed. We need to learn to take responsibility for our own happiness, instead of through shopping, food, sex, alcohol, porn, or Netflix marathons. None of these can make you happy (well maybe sex can). These outside pleasures will only keep you satisfied for a short period of time, and then you will go right back to the same shit you were upset over. You may feel joy and happiness when you think of those things but they won't keep you happy and fulfilled in the long run. You are the one making yourself happy by choosing to think good thoughts of those things. It's your thoughts that are creating how you are feeling.

We can't blame another person for not bringing happiness into our lives. If we do, then we are relying on these people to make us feel good all of the time. Why would we give anyone so much control over us? We can't blame our past for why we are not happy today. If that were the case we would truly be in trouble because we can't change our past, so then we would never be able to be happy. But here's what is so amazing about this: we can absolutely learn to be happy. We just need to change our thoughts about our thinking and then our feelings will change as well. Our past is in the past, we can't change it, so let's leave it there and move into our present and future. Let those feelings go and start creating a new story for how you want to live.

Our thoughts about everything create our feelings, and that is what creates our happiness. How we choose to think of circumstances, or of anything, creates our feelings. We can choose to have bad thoughts about circumstances, or we can choose to have good thoughts about circumstances. It's all in our thinking. Remember, *you're the one in charge of how you feel.* Whatever you decide to think will determine how you feel. You have full control of your thinking, which means you have full control over your own happiness. You are strong, powerful, and have your own mind (which you get to control).

I get asked all the time:

"Christine what inspires you?"
"What have you done to get you to where you are today?"
"How did you make such a huge transformation within yourself in such a short amount of time?"

I learned to take full responsibility for my own happiness, and I know that I am the only one that can create that. Your happiness comes from within, no one else can make you happy but yourself. I realized what would truly make me happy and I committed myself to creating that, not letting anyone stand in the way of me getting what I wanted in life. I took full control. I started reading, listening to podcasts and audiobooks on self-awareness. I closed some doors to friendships that were not healthy and not serving me. I started listening to my Inner Goddess and realized she will never, and has never, let me down.

I learned to appreciate everything in my life, even the circumstances that I didn't like going through. I knew there were reasons I needed to experience what I did and I am grateful for the lessons I have learned. I began to love life and everything around me. I started to become "present in my today" which is extremely rewarding—being able to take everything in at the exact moment as it is happening. Putting the time and effort into working on Me, on Myself, and showing up as that person in the world. I became a Life Coach so I can serve others and watch them grow into who they want to become. I love my life and I love my career. You need to start investing in loving the most important person, which is YOU. How can you give love to someone else if you don't love yourself first? How can you teach someone to love if you don't love who you are? You need to discover self-love—and affirmations are a great place to start.

Affirmations Are the Way to Go

An affirmation is simply a positive statement, word, or phrase that represents what it is you are wanting to believe or create, which you repeat to yourself regularly throughout your day. When you first start saying them, they may sound bizarre and kinda weird, which is totally OK, especially since your Inner Mean Girl doesn't believe them and will try to question your new words becoming your truth. She always tries to get in the way with thoughts like, "You're not skinny, have you looked at yourself in the mirror lately?" or "Money doesn't come your way quickly and easily, look at your bank account . . . BINGO!" or "You're not good at public speaking, you're just going to make a fool of yourself when you get on stage." But just remember that She (your Inner Mean Girl) is your inner child, scared to lose occupancy within you. She doesn't really mean any harm; She just doesn't like change which is why She will try to fight every new thought and positive affirmation that you start wanting to believe. Give it a little time, after saying them to yourself enough times, your subconscious will start to absorb them, and you will eventually feel as if that has always been your reality.

Repeat them out loud to yourself as many times as needed until you feel the truth behind each one. Sometimes some affirmations feel like complete bullshit, there is no possible way that you could automatically start believing that you are your perfect weight, when you have one hundred pounds to lose. Or that you are worthy of love when you have thought for so many years that you aren't. This is completely normal, especially when you are just starting out and opening yourself up to positive self-awareness.

Because our subconscious believes things that we now live by and believe ourselves, we have to retrain the brain by repeating over and over again these new beliefs. Eventually they will begin to manifest and you will believe them as your truth.

If your subconscious is having a hard time believing the new "You" you're wanting to be, you can try a ladder thought like "I am *starting to believe* that I am worthy of other people's love" or "I am *in the process of believing* that I will be my perfect weight of 120 lbs." You can even use "I am *choosing to believe*." You have to build up to those beliefs and slowly retrain your brain to your new truth. These "ladder thoughts" (climbing up the ladder to get to the new thought you want to start believing) will help you believe your affirmations much faster than trying to push through any resistance that you may be having.

Daily affirmations are part of being able to create your dreams. Our subconscious mind listens to everything that we tell it, everything that we say out loud. Whatever is absorbed into the subconscious is what you'll see manifested into your daily life. The subconscious mind is like a bridge between us and the Universe. The best way to reprogram your subconscious mind is through daily repetition of affirmations. Say them in the car, say them while you are getting ready for your day. Set an alarm on your phone to go off that will remind you when to go into full blown, positive affirmations that will literally change your life. Try it for thirty days. You will be blown away.

You can download my list of affirmations at www. christinerizzo.com, just go to the "Affirmations" page.

Saying affirmations are just like going to the gym and working out every day, or hiring a life coach. You need to be consistent; you can't go one or two times and see results. This is a compound effect and over time the shift in yourself starts happening, and eventually you will witness a huge difference in your life. There are multiple apps out there that you can download as well. I use one myself and for my clients so I can send them out weekly affirmations, pertaining to their sessions. By repeating these words of love to yourself, they are going to help change you into the Amazing Woman that you have always been, but are now just learning to love.

Learning to love yourself is such an important part of manifesting what you want into your life. If you don't learn to love yourself first, you will just continue to manifest things that you don't want into your life by default. What we think about, we create.

"I am—the two most powerful words in the Universe.
For what follows them, becomes your destiny."
Unknown

Here are a few examples of the affirmations that I say out loud always with emotion added. When you add emotion, you will automatically raise your vibration which will help you manifest quicker. I say my affirmations a few times a day to help my subconscious believe them faster.

I am love and light
I am one with the Universe
I am one with God
I am one with All
I am enough

I am successful in all areas of my life
I am grateful for my life
I am truth
I am happy
I am healthy
I am abundant
I am the master of my thoughts
I am strong, I am smart, I am sexy
I am generous
I am a master at manifesting
I am worthy of everything that is given to me
I am worthy of all
I am filled with energy everyday

Whatever you put after "I am" will help to reshape your life. After you say these affirmations over and over again, your subconscious will eventually believe them as your truth. Start showing yourself how much you love yourself. Start telling yourself every day that you are an amazing person and you love exactly who you are. No one deserves this more than YOU!

"Be the love that you want to see in the world and in others. Be the example. When you treat someone unkindly with your words and actions, you are treating yourself the same way. We are all One and our energy toward others will only reflect back to us."

Christine Rizzo

You Are Enough

Instead of following our Inner Goddess and our hearts, most of the time we invest in what other people believe we should invest in. ("You have to either be a lawyer or a doctor so you can make the family proud.") We conform to how others believe we should be. ("If you're not 'straight' and are living an alternative sexual lifestyle, then you're going to Hell.") We become ashamed of who we really are, and we start to separate from our true identity. We continue to live our life out of lies instead of out of love for who we are truly meant to be. Until we connect with our true selves and start investing in what is right for us, we cannot live a full, rich, authentic life.

We invest everything we have in believing that we're not good enough. We're not worthy enough, why would anyone love us? It's so crazy that we wind up believing all of these fucked up lies about who we are, what people think of us and how we should be. Self-love is nowhere to be found when we take other people's opinions into consideration. They need to mind their own business so we can all start living our life for who we are and not for how they want us to be.

Many of us go around in our lives trying to be more lovable. We try to make it easy for others to love us. Someone else's inability to love you has nothing to do with you. Your lovability is absolute. Your lovability is already a given, you don't need to change one thing to become more loveable. If you want more love in your life, you have to love yourself. Love yourself even when it's hard. Do this for yourself.

Love is the strongest and most powerful emotion that we can feel, and create in our lives. The question is: *how can you get better at loving yourself?* Because all of us really just want to be loved. When you don't love yourself, you are actually putting out into the Universe that it's OK for others to not love you. Remember, what you choose to give thought to, you create more of. When you put out thoughts of disgust and hate for yourself, you are only bringing more of that to you. When you don't accept yourself, you are not accepting of others. You were created from love; you are made up of love and you are 100% loveable. Love feels great, it feels incredible, and it is available for us to feel anytime we want to feel it.

When you withhold love from yourself it feels horrible, which is what you are doing when you are choosing not to love yourself. Love is for you, love never hurts. Only your thoughts about love do. We often choose not to feel love for ourselves over the lies we continue to feed ourselves with. "I'm not smart enough. I'm not loveable. I'm not worthy of other people's love." When you choose to not feel love, you are only hurting yourself.

We Are All One

This is very, very, important to understand: *there is only one person, which is YOU.* When you hurt someone by acting unkind, rude, or obnoxious, you are hurting yourself. How you treat another person, that is exactly what you will receive back. What you give out, you will get back. There is no other person as far as the law of attraction is concerned. The law of attraction is the law of you, and whatever you feel about anyone else, you are bringing that back to you. Like attracts like. When you judge or criticize someone else, you are judging and criticizing yourself. When you give love and appreciation to someone else, you are giving that back to yourself. What you say to someone else, what you feel toward someone else, what you do to someone else, you are doing it all to you. It's what you give that counts.

The law of attraction is responding to your feelings. It always has and it always will. The other person is you, and you are the other person. We are all one. Pretty intense I know. But if you understand that we are all one then you may hold back next time you are wanting to call the guy that stood you up "an asshole" and instead be OK with his action because your positive attitude about it helped you to attract the new man that you've started dating.

Love the one you're with

Repeat after me:

I Love Myself. Period.

The F-Word Will Set You Free

"Holding a grudge doesn't make you strong; it makes you bitter. Forgiving doesn't make you weak; it sets you free."

Dave Willis

Did she just say the F-word??? Did I just hear her say that I need to "*forgive*" the people from my past to move forward in my life, so I can feel free? Yes, the F-word will set you free by completely forgiving yourself, everyone in your past and everything that has ever happened to you since you were born. I know this sounds pretty crazy having to forgive those that have hurt you in so many ways. But I am here to tell you, that if you continue to hold these grudges from your past, you will continue to prevent yourself from being able to create the life you want.

Forgiveness is like water: we need it to survive. Let go of the pain that has been hurting you for so long, let go of what that person may think or feel. Holding onto anger will only give you negative thoughts and when we think negatively, we will only attract that back to us. So, let's start learning to let that shit go. I mean who really cares what they think? Seriously. Does it really matter? No, not really. What matters is taking care of yourself. When you learn to love yourself enough to let go of the shitty situation that you have been holding onto, you can finally move forward and start feeling more peace in your life. Then you will finally be set free.

Forgiving isn't about being nice to them—it's about being nice to you. It's about putting your need to feel good in front of your need to be right. It's about taking responsibility for your own happiness instead of depending on others to create that for you. It's about owning your feelings and taking back your power by letting go of your hurt, resentment and anger. It's time to say goodbye to your Inner Mean Girl and start letting your Inner Goddess lead the way.

When we don't forgive, we stay stuck in our past and we are not able to move forward. We relive all our bad moments, by holding on and choosing to not let go. Some of us won't even rest until we get back at the other person, hoping to have hurt them as badly as they have hurt us. We will do whatever it is we need to, just so they know how hurt we are at what they did to us. We hold onto the resentment, which keeps us angry, spins us out of control with our thinking, causes depression and creates illnesses in our lives. And we do this for what reason? Just so we can get them back. Hmmm, yeah that feels really good. It feels even better when we wind up in the doctor's office with a terminal disease, because we didn't want to let go of the anger we had for those few people that we felt screwed us over years ago.

Choosing not to forgive, ends up feeling terrible. I know because I have been there many times. Holding onto the anger, thinking that I am hurting the other person, meanwhile I am really only hurting myself. I am the one feeling the emotions, I am the one constantly feeling the anger anytime someone mentions their name. They can't feel what I am feeling, they aren't in my head able to hear my thoughts about them. I mean why do we even let ourselves think about them? Seriously, ask yourself that question again. We wind up continuing to have a relationship with the people we can't stand, all because we don't want to let go. If you think about it, it's so insane! We are self-inflicting ourselves by holding onto our anger. When we hold onto resentment, it's like we are pouring salt onto our wound. We are the only one feeling the pain.

> *"To forgive is to set a prisoner free and discover that the prisoner was you."*
>
> **Lewis B. Smedes**

When we choose to forgive, we can see more clearly, we can breathe easier, we can move on from our past and start creating what we want in our lives. When we forgive, we have learned to love who we are enough to let go so we can be happy. When we forgive, we finally feel what freedom feels like. And Ohhh, it feels so damn good.

Wipe the Slate Clean

Once you have decided to forgive the person, learn to then let it go. Don't hold onto it anymore, don't think about it, don't dwell on it, not one tiny bit. And don't ever question if you did the right thing or not. *Because yes, what you did was right by doing right by you.* By loving yourself enough to give yourself that gift. Remember, forgiving isn't for the other person, it's for you. By forgiving someone, you're not condoning what they did. You are letting go for yourself. Wipe the slate clean. Don't automatically assume that the person is going to hurt you again. When you think like that, you will likely get hurt again. Whatever we put thought to, we create. That is the exact reason why we keep attracting the same situations into our lives.

Let me give you an example. Say you happen to think that men are all liars and cheaters, all because your past boyfriend really hurt you by screwing you over. He cheated on you, multiple times with other women (maybe even a few men) and you wound up with herpes. After ten years, you still haven't forgiven him as you are reminded how much of a loser he is every time you have a flare up (Bastard). With that being said, you can't seem to figure out why you have a hard time meeting a nice guy, one that you can trust. Never putting into consideration how you truly feel about them (that all men are losers). What keeps happening is, that whenever you meet a guy that you are interested in, you automatically start to act a certain way and sabotage the relationship.

You immediately don't trust anyone because of your past experience with that loser ex-boyfriend. You start acting graspy and desperate in your new relationships, obsessively calling and texting. You start arguments, wanting to check their phone to see if they are talking to other women. You wind up attracting the same type of men that do cheat on you because they would rather be with someone else, than be with someone that is CRAZY!!! You are doing this all to yourself by bringing your past issues into your present relationships. And you will show up this way every single time until you learn to let go and forgive. This belief of yours that was created from your past is still affecting you today. And you are proving your beliefs to be true. What you choose to think becomes your truth, it becomes your story. You my friend, are the creator of your story. What you say and believe will always be your truth. There's no getting around this, until you change your story.

Forgiveness stems from love, from learning to love yourself. Through an expression of love and not an expression of fear, we're able to create more peace within ourselves. Our Inner Mean Girl holds onto the fear of possibly getting hurt again, so She holds you back from wanting to forgive.

She is super sneaky in many ways and will stop you from creating the peace you can have within yourself. She knows without fear in your life, She won't exist anymore. And She ain't gonna let that happen so easily. She will pitch every excuse as to why you shouldn't forgive this person. She's no fool. She will throw a temper tantrum, kicking, screaming, and yelling to get your attention so She can stop you in your tracks. She knows exactly how to get her way to keep you under her control. She doesn't care, as She is only out for the one and only . . . HERSELF. She is protecting her domain where She has been living since you were little. Controlling your thoughts, instead of you being able to take the reins. Your Inner Goddess on the other hand is madly in love with you and only wants what is best for you. She could care less what anyone else thinks. She wants you to be happy because She truly knows that your happiness is all that really matters. She is pure love, to your Inner Goddess, it's all about you, because She knows that we are all one.

Let That Shit Go

When we choose to forgive, we are releasing the person that we have been holding hostage within us. Each time you forgive someone, you choose love over fear. You are letting go of your old ways and making shifts toward a happier life. You are letting go and learning to allow. You are letting go of expectations of how you think everyone should be. When we hold onto anger, we are kept prisoners to our pain and we are keeping our feelings from our past alive. Let go of what is in your control (your thoughts) and start to enjoy your life.

I have my clients create a Forgiveness List where they write down 10–15 situations from their past that they remember having negative experiences from. This is a great way to start letting go, you should try it. Keep the list going until you can't think of anything else. Here are a few examples to get you started.

1. When my mom and sister laughed at me when I told them I wanted to be a dolphin trainer when I was younger.

2. When my father drove me and my family in the car when he was drinking throughout the day.

3. I blame my parents for not being there for me when I was younger by not listening to what I needed to tell them.

4. When my friend wasn't there for me when I needed a place to stay.

5. When the kids drive me crazy and I yell at them more than I should.

6. I am angry at myself for never telling anyone no. I always say yes, even when I don't want to do the things they want me to. Then I feel resentful.

7. When I knew one of my close friends went behind my back telling my husband things that weren't true, because she liked him more than a friend.

8. I am angry with myself for eating too much when I know that I shouldn't have and not sticking to my diet.

Once you have written your list out, I want you to go over each situation and really feel the feelings. How do they feel? Do some of them still feel hurtful or negative? If you answer yes, then this is a great way to understand and discover what you are needing to release. You need to clear the negative energy surrounding you. By releasing and letting go, you will stop attracting similar experiences.

Practice Makes Perfect

There is an ancient Hawaiian practice that I want to share with you. I use this practice myself when I feel I need to forgive and let go. It is super effective and is a miracle worker in forgiveness. It is called "Ho'oponopono." There are four steps or phrases that are used and the meaning behind each phrase is this:

"I'm sorry" . . . I acknowledge the situation and I am sorry for holding onto it for so long. I will no longer let this affect me.

"Forgive me" . . . I will release this from myself and it is no longer my issue. I will no longer let this situation affect me.

"Thank you" . . . Thank you for all the lessons I have learned through this situation.

"I love you" . . . I am sending love to the situation which will allow myself to heal and get through this. Love heals all. Love is our only solution.

When we send out love, only love can and will come back to you. "Love attracts love." Thoughts of love toward others will always attract love toward you. The more love you give, the more love you will receive. This practice will help to clear up the negative energy to stop attracting the same negative experiences in your life. With each negative experience you find yourself going through, try and practice this ancient way of forgiveness. Once you apologize, forgive, thank, and love, not only will you feel a sense of clarity, you will feel a heaviness and a feeling of freedom release from your soul. We all deserve to be happy and that can and will be achieved by loving yourself so much that you can forgive. Start today by letting go!!!

Now go over your Forgiveness List that you wrote out, and after each number, read it aloud and then say, "I forgive you, I'm sorry, thank you, I love you. Once you have gone through the forgiveness process, ask yourself:

How do you feel?

If you're upset that is OK. You are detoxing all the negative energy that has been manifesting inside of you for years. Be patient, healing can take some time. Love yourself so you can learn to let go, be happy, and more at peace. Remember, you are in control of how you want to feel. Continue practicing the F-word every day, Forgiveness will completely reform your life in a way that you have never seen before.

Love the one you're with

Repeat after me:

I will learn to forgive myself and others. Always.

Your Inner Goddess

"Don't try to comprehend with your mind. Minds are very limited. Use your intuition."

Madeleine L'Engle

Your Inner Goddess = Your Intuition (Your Higher Self, Sixth Sense, God's Voice, Spiritual Guide, Third Eye . . . Whatever you believe or want to call it. I will also be referring to your Inner Goddess as "She").

This is the voice that screams intuitive loving thoughts and tells you to run in the other direction of fear. This is the voice that protects you when She knows that if you go through with a decision that She has been warning you about, that it will be the biggest mistake of your life. This is the voice that guides you in the right direction, even when you are wanting to head in a different one. She is the voice that tries to keep you back, because She knows the outcome of the direction you want to head in isn't good.

When your Inner Goddess is talking to you, you need to PAY ATTENTION. You need to hear what She is trying to tell you and you need to listen. So many times, we don't want to. We want to do it our way, because our Inner Mean Girl thinks She knows what is best for us. But really your Inner Goddess is the one that knows what is best for you. She is your connection to source energy, She is the one you can trust. She is your Higher Self, and She will never fail or let you down. Your Inner Goddess is always from love, so you need to follow and trust what She is telling you.

When you meet the right person, or find the right house, or go to an interview and you are so sure that you got the position, you just know because it feels so right. There are no questions, it is the feeling of truth. Those are signals from her. That is your Inner Goddess. She gives you this guided feeling within yourself that you experience. Those feelings help you to know when something feels right, or when something feels completely wrong. Your Inner Goddess knows all the answers. She is the one you connect with during meditation, through prayer or whenever you need direction. Your Inner Goddess is your girl, you can count on her, because She will always have your back no matter what. She is there for you, She loves you and She will always take care of you.

By being aware of the signals that She sends to you, you won't wind up making the mistakes that can set you back from getting to where you are wanting to be. When you are aware of your Inner Goddess being present, you are in a state of knowing, and you can comprehend more easily, because you never have to inquire. There is never any doubt. You receive little nudges leading you in the right direction, to do certain things, to think a certain way, or to go to a place that you weren't even thinking about going to. You go and end up meeting your soul mate. (Who knew?) Maybe you were being nudged to take a different route to work, and then hours later you hear there was an accident on the road that you usually travel down. Going the other way helped you to not be a part of the five-car pile-up and saved you quite a bit of money, or maybe she saved you from being late to work from sitting in gridlock.

These little nudges that you experience feel automatic, so you usually don't even pay attention to them. You know those feelings that you get when something deep inside of you is telling you that every time you were with your significant other it just never felt right. You wound up getting a terrible feeling in your stomach, but you didn't want to listen. That was you Inner Goddess wanting to save you from the heartache that She knew you were going to go through, but you didn't listen. And the bastard wound up breaking your heart.

Everyone has the ability to connect with their Inner Goddess. God happened to create us all with an inner guidance system that communicates with us through our emotions. We were created to feel positive and negative emotions for our own protection. When you think of something that gives you warm fuzzy positive, wonderful feelings, you instinctively know that you should keep doing whatever it is that is giving you those wonderful feelings.

We all love feeling good, we are meant to feel good, and that is why we have good feeling emotions. That is your signal from your Inner Goddess to keep doing what you're doing. Those are also the feelings you want to remember so you can keep your frequency high to attract the things that you want more quickly. Sometimes, you may feel hesitant even with a good feeling emotion. This may be because it is over something you have never done or experienced before. Or maybe you feel nervous since you don't quite know the outcome, but you still feel a nudge to head down that path. That is your Inner Goddess telling you that you need to go for it, step out of that comfort zone of yours and start trusting that she is leading you to where you are wanting to go, even though you have absolutely no clue what she is doing (it's called "trusting the process").

There is a reason why you are being led to travel down a path that you may not want to. Sometimes we need to go through some discomfort to get to our end result. The result that we have been wanting for so long. It doesn't just get handed to you, sometimes we need to grow to get to where we want to be. Let me give you an example. You are the lead singer in a rock band called the "Screaming Vagina's". You started out in your garage with your friends and played for years trying to get gigs all around town. Finally, everyone knows who you and your bandmates are because you have played in like every single bar in a ten-mile radius of your hometown. You start getting more known, and now managers are wanting to work with you from all over and want to book you in bigger and better venues. You're a bit intimidated over starting to have fans and becoming more popular since you really are an introvert. The big stage kinda freaks you out.

Your Inner Mean Girl (ego) is wanting to hold you back a bit because the garage and local bars were fun and comfortable for you. But you have always wanted to make it big, you have always seen yourself as this huge rockstar touring the world and living large (private jets, five-star hotels, VIP rooms, champagne and caviar). Your fears are holding you back but your Inner Goddess is wanting to lead you in the direction you are wanting. She is the one that helped lead you to meeting your manager at the hot yoga class you took that day when you weren't even planning on going, but something told you out of nowhere to go. You just need to let go of the outcome and start trusting that She will help get you to where your desires are, where they have always been. You just need to notice her signals and trust that She is doing what She knows best. Guiding you towards everything that you want that is out of LOVE.

When you feel negative emotions—maybe over a situation that is happening, over a job, or a relationship that you are in, or over the person you hired to do work on your house—when you sense those uncomfortable feelings that are telling you something just isn't right, it's time to RUN as fast as you can in the other direction. It's time to let the contractor go that is doing work on your house, because little do you know, he is never going to wind up finishing the job, since you were kind enough to pay him in full two weeks before the job was finished.

That feeling that you were getting when you were writing out the check, something was telling you not to, but you felt bad because he said he really needed the money so he could feed his kids. He lied and never came back to do the rest of the work. When we listen to our emotions, they help save us from the pain, hurt, or stress that we would otherwise have gone through. I personally have had quite a few experiences of not listening to my Inner Goddess as I am sure you have as well. So much unnecessary pain was felt because I chose to ignore what She was trying to tell me. It's about surrendering your control and paying attention to her signals. If you want to live the life that you have always dreamed of, you need to get out of your head and pay attention to your emotions.

She Knows Best

It wasn't until a few years ago that I started to really listen to my Inner Goddess more than ever. Occasionally I would, when I felt a really strong signal, but other than that I wasn't really aware of her signals because I wasn't paying attention. I was so wrapped up in my thoughts, that I would miss what She was trying to tell me. I wanted to do things my way, and that got me into a bit of trouble throughout my teen years and into my 20s.

Junior year in high school, I didn't want to listen to my Inner Goddess during a final exam. She was telling me that She thought it was a really bad idea if I cheated off Scott (names have been changed) who sat in front of me, who cheated off Carolyn who sat in front of him. Yup we all ended up in summer school that year. I didn't need to cheat, I just wanted to because I knew I could. My Inner Goddess was telling me the whole time "Christine don't do it, you're going to regret this, don't do it. You know the answers, let's be smart about this." I didn't listen and it affected my whole summer. I was stuck in summer school, while all my friends were hangin' at Jones Beach, Field 4. Taking in the sun, with the radio blasting, sipping on wine coolers, big hair don't care, electric blue eyeliner and lip gloss #44 perfectly applied to their lips. Packed in like sardines with the rest of Merrick, Bellmore, Wantagh, Seaford and Levittown. Yeah, maybe summer school wasn't so bad after all. So not true, I wanted to be there with them all. If only I listened to my Inner Goddess.

When you become aware of the signals you are receiving through your feelings, it will help to give you clarity knowing that you can control your outcome. Our Creator loves us and only wants good in our lives. Your Inner Goddess wants you to be happy and aware that you are in control of the direction that you want to go in, as long as you learn to listen to her. Meditation will help to strengthen your awareness of listening to your new best friend (IG) more clearly. Once you get good at listening to her, so much happiness will be created in your life, and you will learn to have full control of your destiny.

The Gatekeeper To Your Dreams

Meditation practice is just that—it takes practice. Not once, not twice but over and over again. When I started to meditate regularly, I noticed how much better it made me feel. I noticed these amazing shifts that I started to have in my life. I was able to think more clearly, and I was able to remember things so much quicker than I usually did. Solutions to problems became instinctive. I learned how to connect with my spiritual guide through meditation and I was able to find out answers to questions that I have always wanted to know. Meditation is about being present and being still. It's about connecting to source energy. The more practiced you become at being present and connected to your Higher Self, the more available you are to come up with ideas and take on opportunities that you may miss out on if you are all stuck in your head with mindless chatter.

When we get stuck in our heads, we miss out on what is available to us right now in the moment. Stop and look around you right now. What do you see? What sounds do you hear? Can you hear yourself breathing? Can you hear the wind blowing? Can you hear the traffic or the train going by? Are you sitting down on your couch? What do you feel? Can you feel the softness of the blankets that are around you? Can you feel the fabric of the couch? How does it feel? When we pay attention to being in the "now" and not in our heads, there are no problems. All of the problems that we worry about are in our future. They haven't even happened yet. We don't even know if they are going to happen, yet we continue to worry regardless, all because of the unknown which is out of our control and always will be. When we become more present with what is around us, we are more aware and closer to our creator. When in the now, you can just "be." Living moment to moment, happy as a butterfly. Fluttering around thinking of nothing but flying and looking as beautiful as you are.

As adults, we have high-stress careers, we have bills to pay, families to care for (that can sometimes be high maintenance, like teenage daughters). Our minds are so used to running all over the place having to do everything that is needed to do to take care of everyone, that we rarely find time to do anything that we need for ourselves. We need to stop and let our minds rest; we need to take in what is around us. We need to slow down and learn to meditate by connecting with our Inner Goddess. The more time you spend in the moment, the richer your life will become. By being present, it will get you out of your head, and connect you to source energy. It will raise your frequency, which will then attract the same frequency level to you so you can experience the life that you have been wanting to experience. The life you have always wanted.

I used to think saying affirmations was ridiculous and they would never work. I was wrong. I thought meditation was equally odd, for weirdos and felt that anyone that could sit still for that long and think of nothing, had way too much time on their hands. I always thought meditation was a complete waste of time where I wouldn't be able to get those minutes back and I could be doing something much more productive than listening to meditation music, repeating mantras, with my eyes closed, legs crossed, palms up, deeply inhaling and exhaling. It just made absolutely no sense to me.

Then one day after reading up on meditation and how it changes people's lives, I knew I had to try it. So, I downloaded a meditation app, started with a guided meditation, and then eventually moved to unguided. I am one of those few people that have a hard time with being visual. In a few of the apps that I downloaded, they wanted me to see what they were saying, which didn't work for me, so I moved to the unguided meditations which I happen to like better. I was uncomfortable at first, not really quite sure what to do or what was going to happen. I took baby steps, five minutes my first few times, which led to ten minutes, then I went up to fifteen and then twenty. Some days I can go longer than others, and some days while meditating, my mind is not wanting to turn off, so I cut my session short. And that is OK, I am not hard on myself over it. As you grow through your practice, you may move toward complete stillness and silence. There is no right or wrong way, whatever works for you, as long as you're trying.

"Meditation is not a way of making your mind quiet. It is a way of entering into the quiet that is already there—buried under the 50,000 thoughts the average person thinks every day."

Deepak Chopra

During my meditations I pray first by setting my intentions and then I quiet my mind to connect with my spirit guide and with source energy. When we are meditating, we are listening to the answers to our prayers, we are given inspiration and we are sending out love to the world. Through meditation, my best book ideas and words to be written in this book came to me, when I completely silenced my mind. Our minds race at a thousand miles per hour thinking thousands of thoughts per day. This is one of the reasons why I turned to meditation, knowing I needed to release my thoughts and shut my brain off. I am now able to think more clearly, with such a clear vision of the direction I need to take in my life. I have become infatuated with meditating and I know I could never live without listening to what my Inner Goddess is telling me.

Being In The Now

When you learn to turn off your mind, your Inner Goddess will be able to speak to you. This is where our visions come from, source energy and our Higher Self. You won't always have messages sent from your Guide or from God during the meditation, a lot of times they will come later that day or later that week. A lot of people talk about messages coming to them in the shower. Mine come to me in the middle of the night. Not really the best time, though I am super grateful for them coming to me whenever they do. The Universe doesn't know time. It has no idea when the middle of the night is. Meditation isn't the action, it's the start of the action taking place. It's the signal from the Universe letting you know that your mind is thinking clearly and that you are ready to listen. Meditation helps to push you to take the action. You are setting the intention through meditation to receive guidance. It comes whenever the Universe decides the perfect moment is for you.

How can we learn to quiet our minds so we can feel more in control of our lives?

- *Learn to be in the now. Take everything in around you and be silent for a few moments.*
- *Meditate in the mornings to help set your intentions for the day.*
- *Let yourself be "One with God," "One with the Universe," and "One with All."*
- *Ask for peace, love and harmony while in your meditation. You will always receive what you ask for when it is from the energy of love.*
- *By opening yourself up and connecting with a higher power every day, you are gaining insight to a more peaceful and happy life.*

- *Take this time for yourself by learning to quiet the mind. Stop letting your thoughts control you. Learn to control your thoughts, because YOU are the one in control of what you think.*

  We all deserve to live a fulfilled life of abundance, love, and happiness.

Love the one you're with

Repeat after me:

I Love My Inner Goddess and She loves Me.

Your Vibes Speak Louder Than Your Words

"If you want to find the secrets of the universe, think in terms of energy, frequency, and vibration."

Nikola Tesla

I know one day I am going to die. It's inevitable. (I mean we are all going to die, so why do so many people freak out about it?) How, when or where? I have absolutely no idea, and it doesn't really matter, because it's out of my control and it's none of my business. I don't need to know those answers. I don't want to know those answers. I just know that I am at peace with this, and I'm not scared. It's going to happen one day, and I am OK with that.

I am choosing to not let every fact about what is happening in our world today control my thinking. I get to control that (which is all we can control, as we have figured out throughout the book). We can only control how we want to think about what is going on today. So, I have decided that I am going to show up in the world with who I want to be and how I want to feel every single day. With a positive attitude, knowing that one day, yes, I am going to die. I am not fearful about it. I am fearless.

Understanding that this is all I can control, helps to keep me calm, and content in whatever circumstances are put in front of me. Learning to live in the present, in the now, where there is absolutely nothing to worry about. There is nothing to stress over. It is only when we start to think about the future, or the unknown, (which is out of our control), that we get anxious, worried, and fearful. I have chosen to not let circumstances around me take over my mind and cause it to spiral out of control. I have chosen to not let what other people say affect me.

Constantly obsessing over what is out of our control is not serving you, or anyone around you. What we think about today, we create tomorrow. If you constantly continue to fill your head with the news and what is out of your control, you are creating more of that in your future. More noise, more negativity, and more illness. I am not saying that what is happening around us isn't sad and tragic—coronavirus, rape, murder, modern day slavery to name a few—it definitely is. I am just not letting it control my thinking. I am not obsessing over what I cannot control.

What we think about, we attract into our lives. The energy you are creating from your thoughts is attracting the same energy level back to you. This is why it is so important to understand the energy that you are emitting out into the world will always attract every person, circumstance and life situation that is on *the same energy level that you are on*. This is exactly why people that are always in a bad mood and angry, constantly have life situations and circumstances in their life that are negative. They are never happy and are always complaining. The exact opposite is true with people who are always positive, happy, and kind toward others. Things always go their way. You think it's because they are just lucky, but this isn't the case at all. They are emitting positive energy by their thoughts, and they are attracting all the same people and circumstances to them that are on their frequency level.

Your story becomes your perception through your eyes. We all choose to see things differently. This is why some people act calmer over things that are out of their control and others can't stop obsessing over them. Choose to think about all the positive things that are happening in your life right now instead of the negative. And if there aren't any positives, well then, it's time to really change how you think about things. *There has to be something good in your life*. Hey, I know one . . . YOU'RE ALIVE. Your thoughts and beliefs dictate your reality, so if you want to change your reality, you have to change your beliefs. There ain't no other way to do it. Which means you have to get rid of those beliefs that have been holding you back, because that is why you are where you are today, stuck and unhappy. If you truly believe that you suck at relationships, or that you are broke as shit, or that you are fat and can never lose weight, or that marriages never last, that is your truth. And it will always be your truth, if that is what you believe. Remember, everything that you want and desire is already here, you just need to shift your perception so you can start manifesting it into your life.

Keepin' Those Vibrations High

You may spend a lot of time worrying whether you will ever meet someone that is going to make you happy (but we already know, that doesn't exist, only you can make yourself happy) or if you are going to get the job that you want so badly. You spend time worrying because you don't have full faith in yourself, and you just don't trust that it's possible. With negative thoughts, comes negative energy that you are putting out into the Universe. To get the job, or the partner you're wanting so badly, you have to create positive energy, and have faith that it will happen. Remember like attracts like. Therefore, the energy that is vibrating inside of you, will always attract similar energy back to you.

Let's talk about our feelings, as they are super important to creating and manifesting what you are wanting. Women get so much shit for being overly emotional, which can be true at times, (OK so we can be super hormonal some months too . . . And???) but this is actually an asset, because our feelings are what makes us powerful manifestors. Why are feelings so important for manifesting you ask? *Because how you feel and see your future will predict what your future will actually end up looking and feeling like.* You will learn how to purposely imitate the feelings that you need to feel to manifest the life you are wanting to create.

Take a quick second right now and get in touch with your feelings. How do you feel today, right at this very moment? Are you happy? Worried? Stressed? Excited? Bitchy? (Maybe it's that time of the month.) How we feel day-to-day determines what we will manifest and create in our lives. Being able to create the life you want to live feels really good to you, right? (I mean, how could it not? You are learning that you are a powerful badass and you can create whatever you want.) It's not really about what you will create that is going to make you happy. It's the *feeling* of having the life that you have always wanted that you're actually after. How would having the life you have always dreamed of feel to you? Exciting? Fun? Adventurous? Ecstatic? Romantic? Sexy? Empowering? Freeing? You have to go after the feelings of what it would feel like to have the life you have always dreamed of. You have to imagine how that life is going to make you feel. You want to feel good and feeling good comes from within, but to manifest your desires you need to feel like you already have what you are wanting. You need to envision as if you are already living that life. You have already put it out into the Universe, which means your manifestation process has already taken place. Now it is up to you to bring it into physical form using your feelings of already having it.

What are those feelings that come up for you when you think of the life you are wanting to create? What are your five biggest feelings that you will feel when you will be living the life you have always wanted? Write those down in a journal right now. Come on, go get a piece of paper or your journal so you can write down those feelings. I can wait, I'm not going anywhere. Now you need to start feeling those five feelings every day. The more you feel them, the quicker the Universe works to bring you more things into your life that will keep you feeling those feelings. Feeling those feelings everyday will eventually help you to create whatever it is you want. Like attracts like, so you have to keep feeling those feelings to create. That's why I wanted you to write them down, so now you can practice those exact feelings every day. You're welcome.

The Law Of Attraction = Like Attracts Like

Positive energy is attracted to positive thoughts and feelings, as negative energy is attracted to negative thoughts and feelings. If you think shitty thoughts and you feel shitty feelings, you are going to attract a shitty life. If you think amazing thoughts and you feel amazing feelings, you are going to attract an amazing life. Your outer experiences are the exact reflection of your inner thoughts and feelings. So, you need to start cleaning out the thoughts in your head that are creating the life that you are living today, and you need to start creating new thoughts that will help you to create the life that you have been wanting to live.

We wind up carrying a lot of negative energy around with us when we hang out with the wrong people. If you happen to be bffs with Negative Nelly, who is always complaining about everything in her life from the sky not being blue enough, to the person standing in line in front of her that was taking way too long when they were ordering, then I would suggest you find yourself a new best friend. Misery loves company. She will only keep dragging you down, and she definitely won't support your new way of thinking. If you need to find some new friends, then hop to it, so we can get this new life of yours started. Stop letting what other people say affect you. That is their story not yours. Walk away from the conversation if you're feeling the energy shift from positive to negative. Protect your energy by not listening to anything or anyone that doesn't feel positive. The energy that we put out into the world is affecting not only you but those around you. We are all magnets because we are made of energy. What you give out, you will always receive back.

Your perception of what is happening in your life today, is how you are choosing to think of what is happening. Your perception becomes your truth and shows you exactly what you are seeing. It's your story. If you live in a scarcity mindset, of fear, helplessness, and worry, then that is exactly what you will wind up creating and that is what will be shown to you. When you learn to see things from a place of abundance, love and faith knowing that the Universe is always going to give you what you are wanting, you will feel much more relaxed and content. You will be able to breathe, knowing and trusting that everything is going to be OK. It's all about how you choose to see things.

> *"You have to get uncomfortable. If not, you'll never move. Elevate. On to—not better things. Not the next best thing. On to higher frequencies."*
>
> **Jill Telford**

The people we surround ourselves with are mirrors for who we are and how much or how little we love our self. We attract people into our lives for a reason; to learn from them. The people that we attracted to us, have attracted us to them as well. I know this may sound ridiculous, but that is how it works, so hear me out. We are all made of energy and we are all on certain frequency levels. We attract the same people that are on the same frequency level that we are on. It's the same as how radio stations work, they are on frequency levels too. We can't turn on 95.5 which happens to be a jazz station and expect today's hits to play. Today's hits is playing on 105.1 which is on a different frequency level.

Keepin' Yo Frequency High

When your vibrations are high and you're on a high frequency level, you're in a good mood, you have good feelings throughout the day of happiness, love and maybe even thoughts of feeling grateful. With those good thoughts and feelings, you are attracting that exact frequency level back to you. You will wind up running into people that are really nice, you don't have to wait in a long line at the grocery store, every light you come to automatically turns green and there wasn't any traffic that day. Things just happened to go your way. Those were not coincidences (there's no such thing), they happened because you were on a high frequency level and you were attracting those people and situations to you. You can have days like that every day if you choose to. You just have to keep your vibrations high.

When your vibrations are low and you're on a low frequency level, your day tends to not be that great. Maybe you woke up and tripped on a shoe getting out of bed, which set your mood for the rest of the day. You spilt coffee on your shirt that morning, and then one thing after the other goes wrong. All because you started out on a low frequency level and didn't change your thoughts to get yourself onto a higher frequency and out of the mood you were in. So your day wound up continuing that way. You can change your day anytime by recognizing what is going on and by changing your thoughts about it. To change your frequency to a higher level, start thinking about what makes you happy.

Put on music that you love and start singing as loud as you can, compliment a few people that you run into that day, or maybe call a friend that is always in a good mood, so some of their mojo will rub off on you. It's really pretty simple, it just takes some practice to notice your thoughts around the circumstance so you can change them. Here's a challenge for you. If someone who is at a lower frequency than you comes toward you and tries to change how you're feeling that day, show them love (compliment them). You will help change their frequency, as well as your own. It will bring you to an even higher frequency. Whenever you raise another person's energy level, you will get that brought back to you a hundred times more. Just by "spreadin' the love."

The best way to get your frequency level high is by setting your day to be happy and filled with love every morning. Start by waking up and being grateful. Before you get out of bed, tell the Universe what you are thankful for. Every day before my feet touch the ground, I thank the Universe for waking up and being grateful that I am alive today and that I am healthy.

Here are a few examples of the gratitudes that I say every day, in no particular order. You can write your own as well, with whatever resonates with you.

Thank you for:

- *My home*
- *The Electric Co. (I actually like to thank the people that help run it every day for us as well)*
- *The fresh water that we get to drink everyday*
- *The food that we have in our refrigerator and pantry*
- *The clothes in my closet*
- *The birds that I get to listen to every morning*
- *The trees that give us oxygen to breathe everyday*
- *My health*

- *My life*
- *My family*
- *My business*
- *The money that I have in my bank account*
- *The career I am creating*
- *My clients*
- *My happiness*

Even if we don't have as much as we would like to have in our lives, we need to be thankful for what we do have to be able to bring more of what we are wanting. You have to be thankful for what you already have.

Ways To Keep Those Vibes High

- *Listen to some music and dance like you have never danced before. Make a playlist or download some music from iTunes. And just dance, dance, dance, like no one is watching.*

- *Be thankful for whatever you have in your life and everything you are asking for. The more grateful you are, the more the Universe responds.*

- *Surround yourself with positive like-minded people. And make sure they love to boogie too, so you can all start dancing on tables together.*

- *Fill your soul with things that you love doing.*

By staying on a high frequency of happiness, love and gratitude, you will see your life change dramatically.

The Keys To Your Power

Love and gratitude are the keys to your power, to receiving the life you are meant to live. Each of these keys hold the power within you. Love being the first and the most dominant in your life. You must learn to love like you have never loved anything before. (This isn't always easy, but trust me, this is what you need to do.) Look around you, what do you see? There has to be something around you that you love? Start falling in love with life, notice what you see that you love and tell yourself, "Oh my gosh I love that! I love the sun when it's shining, I love the house that I live in, I love the sound of rain, I love going out to dinner, I love my friends, I love my family. I love those Jimmy Choo shoes, I love the Louis Vuitton purse that is going to be mine one day. I love traveling around the world. I love the fact that I am a badass and I have the power to create the life I want to live."

There is no fucking limit to the love that you can feel. It's limitless and it's amazing because you get to feel all those feelings. Who wouldn't choose to love everything around them? The ultimate power of love is to fall in love with everything around you, to fall in love with life. I know this can be difficult at times, especially if you are not in a good place in your life. But you have to learn to do this, if you want to be able to create what you want in your life. Without love, you will just stay where you are, creating the things that you don't want. So, I am telling you to start doing this, because it is one of the most important keys to your power.

Gratitude is the second highest vibration (love being Numero Uno) that you can put out into the Universe. Whatever you are grateful for, you will see more of in your life. Whatever you choose to take for granted, you will see less of. You have the choice to either bring more positive or more negative into your life. It's up to YOU. When you are grateful for what you have, you will always be given more. That's just how it works my friends. I hope everyone is paying attention. I am so quizzing you at the end of this book. I am not kidding because I want you to have the life that you deserve. You better be taking notes, or highlighting in this book, I don't care what you do. Just start doing what you need to do so you can start manifesting the life you want, the life you deserve. OK?

Being in a state of gratitude is about having an awareness of and a deep appreciation for the many miracles in your life. When you are grateful for the things in your life, it makes you feel good and those feelings put you on a very high frequency which connects you to source energy. When you are connected to source energy you are in a much more powerful state to manifest more good experiences into your life. By being grateful you are putting out positive energy into the world, which makes the positive energy reflect back to you. This happens with all experiences in our life, and this is why it is so important to be more positive than negative. What we put out we will always receive back. Gratitude is one of the fastest ways to connect to source energy and one of the highest vibrations to manifest quicker.

Learning to appreciate everything in your life is one of the most important aspects to creating the life you want. It's essential to manifesting. Whatever we appreciate, we create more of. When you are in a state of appreciation, you're in vibrational alignment with the universe and with love. What we appreciate, feel grateful for, and send unconditional love to will always multiply in our life. What we focus on by putting thought to, will always increase. What we feel grateful for will always magnify. So, whatever it is you want in your life, you have to first feel grateful for what you already have.

- *Be grateful for everything you have already received in your life (past)*

- *Be grateful for everything that you are receiving in your life today (present)*

- *Be grateful for what you are wanting in your life, as though you have already received it (future)*

If you're not grateful for what you have already received in your past, or for what you have today, then you will never have the power to fully change your today so you can live the life you are wanting. You have to give love by being grateful. You have to start being grateful for your today and for your future as if you have already received what you are wanting. The more you feel grateful, the more love you give and the more love you give, the more you will receive. Every time you feel grateful you are giving love, and whatever you give, you will always receive.

When you are grateful for the things you have, no matter how small they are, you will always receive more of what you are grateful for. If you are grateful for the money that you have, even if it's not a lot, you will receive more money, if you are grateful for the relationships in your life, even if they are not as perfect as you would like them to be, your relationships will get better. Gratitude begins with two simple words—thank you. The more you say thank you the more love you are putting out into the Universe.

When anything good happens to you throughout the day, say thank you. When you find a parking spot, say thank you. When you receive your paycheck, say thank you (and then you can add an additional, there's more where that came from, so you can start believing that is true, which then the Universe will have to provide to you). When you write a check to the electric co., or for your mortgage payment, for your rent, or to your credit cards, say thank you. If it weren't for those companies lending you the money or supplying you with electricity, you would never have the things that you have. Be thankful for paying your taxes, and that you are actually creating enough of an income to have taxes taken out. If you get angry because you have so many bills, you will only attract more bills.

When you bitch and complain over anything, you attract more of what you are not wanting into your life. Give thanks for your health, for your arms, your legs, your fingers and toes. Give thanks to all the men that have built the roads and bridges so we can travel throughout the world. Be grateful for the clothing on your back and the food on your table every night. Be grateful for the bed that you sleep in and the warm cozy blanket that you get to sleep with on those chilly nights. Every day, every second is an opportunity to show love toward what you are grateful for. Do this for yourself, for your happiness, and for everything to multiply in your life. Being grateful costs you nothing. The more gratitude you show, the more abundance you will receive. Because without gratitude my friends, you are pretty much powerless.

When you turn toward love, your life will dramatically change. You will become more alert, you will remember more things, you will become more aware of the things around you and you will feel genuine happiness. Your job is to love as much as possible every day. To turn from the things that you don't love, to not pay attention to anything but feelings of love. Your mind is a powerful tool that you need to learn to control so you can create the life you are wanting, so you can create the life you deserve. Try to notice when your mind is trying to distract you with out-of-control thoughts. That's your Inner Mean Girl not wanting to change. Remember, you are the driver of your mind, you are in control, you are the one in charge, so be aware and pay attention to when negative thoughts try to creep in. Learn to take control, your mind only takes off on its own when you're not paying attention to what you are thinking about.

> *"You cannot exercise much power without gratitude because it is gratitude that keeps you connected with power."*
>
> **Wallace Wattles**

When You Believe, You Will Receive

Now that you know the keys to your power, both love and gratitude, they will help to strengthen your faith. Belief in the unforeseen, but knowing that it exists. Trust is what allows you to take risks. When you were younger and your friends told you to turn around, close your eyes, cross your arms over your chest, and fall backward, trust is what let you fall, knowing that your friends were there to catch you. Faith is what crushes the fear that is inside of you. Learning to believe will not only help transform your life, it will get you to your desired outcome, to where you have always wanted to be. It will give you the confidence knowing that you are the creator of your destiny. No one else but you!

You have to trust that what you are wanting to create (manifest), which isn't there that you can see yet, is going to come to you. If you have any doubt in your mind, that is when you push away whatever you are wanting from coming. What we think about we create. Whatever thoughts we have good or bad we wind up creating. When you don't trust, you are putting those vibes out there, and that is exactly what you get. The opposite of what you want.

I know and always believe that whenever I am looking for a parking spot wherever I happen to be, I will always, no matter what, get a spot. Always, I never doubt. I may have to circle once, but then a spot opens up immediately. This wasn't always true for me. I can tell you stories of me and my sister waiting for parking spots at the outlet malls in Orlando. Oh my gosh we would circle for what felt like forever. Once we even left because we waited more than thirty minutes. I seriously didn't need to shop that badly to wait longer than that. My credit cards at the time must have been feeling the same way, Oh My Gosh! I am just realizing right at this moment, I was the one manifesting us not being able to get parking spots easily. All because I knew the debt I had at the time. I also knew that I would have to hide whatever I purchased from my controlling ex-husband.

Those thoughts of mine at the time had me feeling a certain way even before we got there. I remember saying to my sister on our way there "It's always so hard to find a parking spot, why do we even try? Do we really have to go? I would rather go to the mall where they valet park, can't we go there instead?" I was already putting that negative energy out into the Universe and creating difficulty for us to find any parking. You see when you believe whatever you are telling yourself, you will always create that, and you will always be able to prove it. It is super mind blowing that we have the power to attract whatever it is we want. We just now have to learn how to deliberately create, which you will learn in the next chapter, "Ask and it Will be Given." My story about parking was never true for my mom. She always knew that she would find a spot, no matter if we were at the airport or if we were at The Busy Bee Flea Market. She would always say, "There's a spot for me, I know there is" and minutes later someone was pulling out and she was pulling in.

Here is a great exercise to do which helps you to feel the love for what you already have and what you are asking for. Make it a goal to do this every day. Write down 3–5 things you are grateful for. This is one of the homework assignments that I ask my clients to do when they sign up for my coaching program. Once you are in the flow of gratitude, the Universe brings that love right back to you in so many amazing ways. The higher frequency energy that is put out, the quicker things manifest into our lives. Gratitude is one of your keys to opening the channels to the abundance in your life.

Christine Rizzo

Love the one you're with

Repeat after me:

I am so grateful for everything I have and for the love that I give to myself and to those around me.

Ask and It Will Be Given

"If you don't like the road you're walking, start paving another one."

Dolly Parton

Have you ever thought of a friend and just minutes later, that friend calls you? Been listening to a playlist in your car, thinking about a song that you love, and then it comes on? Or one day you were craving this certain dish from a particular restaurant, and then all of a sudden, your significant other calls you from work saying that they are headed to that exact restaurant for a meeting and wants to know if they could bring you home dinner from there? Coincidence? Nope. You manifested that shit. No joke, totally true. You visualized something and it appeared in your reality. That is how we manifest, see I told you that you are one Powerful Bitch. What you put thought to, you create. Now I am not saying the little things that run through our heads for a few seconds at a time instantly get created into your reality. (Could you imagine? That wouldn't be good at all, and we would probably get into a lot of trouble if that happened, let's not go there please.) I am talking about things that you put more thought to. Everything you imagine, think of, or visualize, has the potential to come into your physical reality. Ding, ding, ding, jackpot! Life doesn't get better than this! Who thought it could be so easy?

Tell me, when you were a child, how often were you caught staring out the window of your classroom? What about when you were a teenager? Quite a bit I am sure. When we were younger, we were so good at visualizing, and unfortunately, we were told that daydreaming was a bad thing to do during school. We were told we needed to pay attention so we could learn things that we hardly even remember today. We would get in trouble and we slowly lost our powerful manifesting skills. We got less and less visually creative as we grew into adults, and we stopped daydreaming altogether. Daydreaming happens to be one of the most powerful components to an incredible future. Most of the successful people in this world daydreamed to create exactly what they wanted in their life.

I want to let you in on a little secret, YOU NEED TO START DAYDREAMING AGAIN! You need to daydream so you can start manifesting the shit out of everything you have ever wanted, and start learning how to intentionally create. You need to, because this is such an important part to manifesting. Seeing it before you actually have it. Visualizing everything that you have ever wanted in your mind. Go fucking big, don't hold back. You have the power to create, so why the hell not go as big as you can. Visualization is one of the fastest ways to bring your manifestations to completion. Everything that has ever been created, started with an idea in someone's mind. Take the Wright brothers who invented the airplane and how to fly. They had an idea, which became a vision, and then they created it. They visualized themselves flying their plane. Professional athletes are trained to do this all the time. They will visualize themselves performing before their season has even started and then they visualize their win. It's not just about training their bodies, it's about learning how to train their minds as well.

Visualizing is about getting very detailed, as detailed and clear in your vision as you can be. The universe needs clarity, it needs to know exactly what you are wanting and asking for. You don't want to ask for a new car and not be specific. A new car to the universe may be a baseline Prius where to you it is a top of the line Maserati. You said new car, the new car came, but it wasn't the exact car that you were really wanting. So, get clear on what you want.

Not everyone is able to visualize that well, and visualizing in the beginning can be a bit more challenging for some than others. If you're having trouble seeing things around you when you close your eyes, then just focus on the feelings that you need to be feeling to create. Feel the happiness, the joy, the excitement of already having what you are asking for. Those are the feelings that are going to help you manifest. Remember, the Universe is responding to the vibration of your feelings, which is always a result of your thoughts. Thoughts create feelings, which then create your results. You want to get on a high frequency so you can create faster. To raise my frequency, I turn to music. I love listening to all kinds of music and I know immediately that my energy level is going to rise quickly. I created a playlist of songs that I can dance to so I am able to raise my vibrations and dance like I am dancing on the bar like when I was in my 20s. Yup those were some fun, and crazy days. Throw on a little Britney Spears radio (don't judge, we so would have been friends if we knew one another back in the day) maybe some JLo, Rhianna, or Lady Gaga, and start shaking those hips like you're auditioning to be a dancer for the Super Bowl halftime show. (Watch a Shakira video, if you're confused, she knows how to shake it.)

It may be easier to manifest by creating a vision board. I have my vision board in my office so I can see it every day. It's your reminder of what you want to attract into your life. This can be a lot of fun because you are creating a visual, which is helping you see what it is that you want to focus on. You can go on Pinterest and print out a bunch of photos of the things that you want or you can look up online how to create a vision board. It's so much fun, picking out whatever you like, and placing your order. This is one of my favorite things to do because it's like having your own personal craft day with the Universe.

Manifesting requires a lot of faith that is not yet seen. It requires us to not only believe in ourselves, but invisible forces, like the power of your Inner Goddess, the Universe, God. These are all the same forces that ensure us that the sun is going to come up every morning, the moon is going to shine at night, the bees are going to pollinate and make honey, the birds are going to keep singing, and the grass is going to keep growing. The same exact force that you my friend are going to learn how to use to become a badass manifesting queen.

On The Other Side Of The Rainbow

Everyone is always telling us to be positive, you have to be positive, just be positive. Every self-help book you pick up they tell you, "Just be positive and you will learn to see things differently." In the fucked up crazy world that so many people think we live in today (which is really only how one perceives it), it's so easy to roll your eyes to the positive and get lost in the negativity. The news telling us that there is not enough of anything in the world and that we are all going to wind up killing one another. Social media friends are constantly complaining. People getting angry over circumstances that they can't control but feel the need to scream it out and share it with all their friends. Magazine and newspaper articles making sure we know that the economy is crashing again. Friends drain us with their problems, asking us to help fix them, and then when we give them advice, they never take it but continue to complain about the same shit over and over again. We all know someone like that. (Friends: you're not allowed to keep bitching about something if you don't do anything about it. Trust me, everyone is tired of hearing the same crap for years, become the adult that you are and take accountability for what is going on in your life.)

We are all human and I know that it is impossible to be positive 100% of the time. I wish I could feed you all these lies and tell you that life really is made up of rainbows and unicorns, and let's throw in some daisies too. That they are all waiting for you on the other side of the rainbow. There is also a lantern waiting for you to rub so you can make three wishes when the genie appears. Sorry, I can't bullshit you, I'm a Sagittarius and we Sag's don't lie. But just because life isn't made of rainbows and unicorns, doesn't mean that we need to give up on ourselves either. We were built to experience different emotions, not just the positive ones. We need to experience all kinds of emotions, both positive and negative. If we weren't then they would never exist. There are important lessons behind these circumstances, and in order for us to grow, we must go through certain experiences in our life so we can evolve. If everything was perfect how would we learn? How would we advance to the next level? We would never be able to, and that is exactly why, every once in a while, life just happens to throw you a monkey wrench. This is all happening for your growth, for you to learn from. No matter what may happen in your life, it is serving a purpose, and that purpose is to evolve.

We need to all learn to be intentional with what we allow ourselves to listen to, read, and watch. Our minds are precious, and we can't always be in control of everything, but that doesn't mean that we need to give up and saturate ourselves in everyone else's victimized world. Including your own. Protecting your mindset and learning to be intentional with what you are choosing to focus on will help you to keep your vibrations high, which will then help you to stay focused on attracting all the amazing things you want into your life. I want to encourage you to take some time away from the negative that has been in your life. Find those sources of negativity that you can control and stop paying attention to them. Change the subject when friends, coworkers, or family members start to complain about anything negative. I like to change the subject by giving someone a compliment. It always works and it usually puts a smile on their face. It definitely helps to change their mood, and they usually always forget what they were just talking about (win-win right there, the negative conversation stopped and you made them feel good). Stop watching the news, it's made up of lies and extreme exaggeration. If you want to believe in lies, choose the rainbows and unicorns, those will serve you better. Don't go on social media as much. Stop following those friends of yours that are constantly negative. You can unfollow them or just hide them (they will never know), but that's up to you.

We may not be able to control everything in our lives, but we can be intentional with most of it. I haven't watched the news in years, I just know that they exaggerate their stories and whatever is happening in the world is out of my control, so why bother? People would say to me all the time "You need to be aware; you need to know what is going on in the world." Actually, NO I really don't. The news is just creating chaos, they are trained to fill our heads with bullshit so they can intimidate us and be in control. Tragedy sells and puts fear in everyone. Sounds so much fun, right??? I choose to live away from fear, and I choose to be happy. Staying away from negative things makes me happier than I have ever been. I can focus clearly and I can keep my vibrations high so I can keep attracting the things I want in my life.

Start becoming aware of who you're spending your time with. Unfollow the people that you know you need to. Our minds are way too precious; they absorb everything we hear, see, and read. Go out of your way to prove to yourself that the world is much more positive than you have been thinking, look at how beautiful the world is around you. Your mind will always end up finding what you're looking for, so start looking for what you want to see, start looking for the beauty, the good in others. Let go of the negative and start creating the happiness that you have been wanting in your life. Remember, when you choose to focus on the negative around you, that is exactly what you will attract back to yourself. You are a magnet and you attract everything that you focus on.

When you believe that everything you desire already exists, you are naturally able to let go of the outcome.

Start living intentionally by setting your intentions every day for how you want your day to go. I do this during my meditation. I will intentionally set my day for how I want it to be. I visualize exactly what I am telling the Universe. We all have the power within us to do this and to expect what we are asking for to happen. When you are so sure about what you want and you expect it, the Universe has to give it to you. What you think and believe, you will receive. You can say to me, "Christine, that is so not true, I have been asking and I believe it's coming but, I am still not getting what I have asked for." Actually, here's the truth, you can fight me all you want, but this is the absolute truth. Gurrl, if you already don't have what you are wanting or what you have asked for, it's only because you don't have the faith that it is really coming, or maybe you don't have the faith that you have the power to manifest. You don't have it because you don't really believe that you can have it or that it will come to you. It doesn't get clearer than that. And if that is the case, you need to do more thought work on your beliefs.

You have to surrender yourself to the Universe. You just need to hand everything over to the Universe and let go. Sit back and allow it all to come to fruition, releasing the grip and trusting that everything is going to work out the way it is meant to. Even if that means you had left your fiancé at the altar, because you finally listened to your

Inner Goddess, surrendering yourself to what the Universe wants for you because little did you know that when you went on your honeymoon alone, you wound up running into your old boyfriend from high school who happened to be single as well, and the two of you have been together ever since. Coincidence, NOPE: a gift from the Universe. It's about letting go of the outcome and letting the Universe do what it is meant to do. When we constantly try to interfere, we throw things off track of what the Universe is trying to bring to us. It's not on our timing of when we want things to happen—and it's not your business when things come into your life either. I'm not saying that you give up on taking action, just loosen the reins that you're holding on tight to, so the Universe can do its job.

Getting Clear on Universal Lingo

- *Be super clear on what you are wanting, I mean crystal clear. Get specific on your desires.*

- *See it, imagine exactly what you want.*

- *Feel it, feel yourself driving the Maserati (go to the dealer and test drive the car so you get the real feel).*

- *Fall head over heels for it, think about it all the time, download pictures of it and use those photos as your screensaver.*

- *Love it, like you already have it. Own it and be grateful that it's on its way.*

- *Believe it, don't question it. Not even one single little "how?" or "when?" Trust and know that what you ask for will come to you.*

- *Allow it, surrender yourself and let the Universe do what it has always done. The only job it knows. Moving circumstances and situations around so you can have whatever it is you are wanting.*

Love the one you're with

Repeat after me:

I believe in myself and I believe that the Universe will always provide what I ask for.

You Are an Ever Evolving Badass

"The whole point of being alive is to evolve into the complete person you were intended to be."

Oprah Winfrey

In December of 2016, a few days away from the ball dropping and from ringing in the New Year, I knew I didn't want to do this for another year. I knew that I needed to break away and to start fresh. I knew that my only way for true happiness was freedom, and I knew what I needed to do. I knew that I needed to set myself free from the pain that I was in for years, and I knew that If I didn't do it now, I was truly going to break. I was so tired of the fighting, I was so tired of feeling angry, I was so tired of the negativity throughout the house, the chaos every day, I was so fucking tired of the abusive words being thrown back and forth like fists swinging in a boxing match.

So, on January 1 of 2017, I made a commitment to myself and I asked my husband of sixteen years for a divorce. I tried leaving a few times, but the timing wasn't right. The girls were way too young, and I wasn't strong enough mentally. We lived this way for many years, and I have to be honest, I was fucking over it. I needed to breathe again, I needed to laugh again, I needed to be happy again, because I was so far from it. I was tired of playing make believe in front of everyone, I was tired of not being true to myself. I was tired of the lies; the many lies that we told one another every day.

I left the marriage, settled for less than nothing, just so I could walk away. I knew that I would one day be able to support myself again, I knew that I had dreams that I wanted to achieve and I knew that I wasn't going to let anyone stop me. What I didn't know was how to get out of the continuous fighting that carried on and off throughout our two and half-year divorce. WTF ??? I was divorcing him for a reason, not to still fight and feel the negative energy. It felt worse than when we were married, and that is when I knew I had to do something. I had to fix this for myself. I knew that I couldn't change him or his actions. I knew that I couldn't make him be someone that he wasn't. And I knew that I needed to change my thoughts about what he may say or do, for me to be at peace with where this was all going.

So, I bought a bunch of self-help audiobooks so I could listen to them when I would go on my walks or whenever

I drove in the car. I listened to the four audio books that I purchased over and over and over again. To the point where I could recite them in my sleep, I wanted the knowledge from them to embed into my brain so I could start living that way as my truth. What I loved so much about relistening, was that every time I played it for a second, third, fourth or even a seventh time, I would hear something new that I missed the original time.

Days into working on myself, my life started to change right in front of my eyes. Things around me started to look more and more beautiful. Things that I never paid any attention to in the past. The world around me was brighter and the colors were much more vibrant. I looked forward to drinking my coffee outside everyday so I could listen to the birds sing and watch them chase one another. I would get a kick out of watching the squirrels act completely crazy. Those silly critters would freeze when they would notice me, then run up the tree as fast as they could. I even had this cute little adorable lizard take up vacancy in my portable grill. I would talk to him every day, (big smile) I even helped him through his shedding stage, making sure he wasn't going through any anxiety of "letting go." I would actually miss seeing him if he left "Casa de Grille" for a few days, worried and hoping he wasn't killed or eaten by one of the feral cats that lived on the block. Then one day I started to question myself. Ummmm . . . What the hell is happening to me? Is this shit for real? Have I been abducted? Can someone please tell me where Christine went? I felt like fucking Snow

White, I felt like I was in a fairytale on acid with this big smile watching the animals run all around.

My truth was changing. My eyes were being opened to what the Universe has given us all: the art of learning how to live in the moment by living in the now. I was taking it all in, and I was so much happier. People around me were nicer, or so it seemed to me. My perception of the world was changing and I loved what I saw. Everything around me started to change drastically for the better and I was loving every moment of it. Friends noticed, saying "Christine you look really happy, you seem different, you look so free!" I was starting to learn how to love myself, and the world around me. And once I understood how to love myself fully, that is when my life really started to shift more than ever.

Change Is Good

We are meant to change. As humans, we were made to grow throughout life. We are made to go through challenges, hardships, and sorrow. We are made to experience LOVE and HAPPINESS. We grow immensely from change, and though change can be difficult, it helps us to grow as humans. If we don't learn to grow, we will just stay the "same," in a place of normalcy because it's comfortable. But unfortunately, most people don't like change, they are scared of it, they feel intimidated by it. I used to think that the unknown can be scary, especially when we have absolutely no control over it. Until my faith deepened, knowing and believing that the Universe will always take care of me. Now, I never question, I just know and believe. And that is exactly what the Universe gives me back in return, exactly what I think.

Understanding that we don't have control over anything but ourselves can be difficult to comprehend. But the truth is that we can only control our thoughts and our actions. What is so amazing about this is that we are able to change how we choose to think about change. We can learn to think that change is good for us, and that it will help us grow which is important for us to do as humans. Or we can stay stuck in our beliefs thinking that change is bad, that we don't like it, and we never will.

I mean why would we want to explore the world? Why would we want to try new things? Why would we want to learn anything different than we already know? (I mean, that takes a lot of fucking energy.) To go back to school so we can start a new career? To move to a new state, town or country because the Universe is pulling you in that direction? Why would we want to do those things when we could just stay where we are doing the same old shit we have always been doing? (Snoooooze BORING!!!) It's time to live a little my friends, it's time to get out of your comfort zone and start dancing on the bar. Let's have fun and start living our lives like we're meant to. Wild and crazy!

I went through quite a bit of change in a short amount of time. I got divorced, I moved three times, I reinvented myself, I started a new relationship (with someone I have known since kindergarten, thanks to good old Facebook, we love you Mark Zuckerberg), I got remarried, he moved from California to Florida so we could be together, we moved in together (lots of change there). I went back to school to start a new career, and all this happened within three years. Trust me I get it. It wasn't easy. It was definitely challenging at times, but I knew that I would grow from what I was going through, and I knew I would eventually find my rainbow. I embraced every moment and I kept telling myself that the Universe has my back, the Universe is going to take care of me, and I never doubted that for one moment.

Workin' On You

Life may not always be easy but that is because we are meant to be challenged so we can evolve. We grow from our experiences, from our achievements, and from our failures. Our lives are meant to be difficult at times. And rewarding as well. When we don't accept change, we wind up feeling more pain throughout our life than when we learn to accept it. If feelings of being uncomfortable have come, or feelings of unhappiness, this is probably the reason why. Your Inner Goddess is sending you signals that it's time for you to evolve. Your mind craves change, so don't suppress the emotions of fear and anxiety, lean into them and take on the challenge. Let them go through you. I can promise you there truly is a rainbow on the other side. I am living proof of it. I have been down that road. You have to push through the obstacles instead of running from them if you want to evolve and feel the freedom that life has to offer.

So many times, we learn to have these fears that we have created because other people have projected their beliefs onto us. No one can decide what is right for you in your life. No one can decide what you should do, or what you shouldn't do. No one can decide how you should be living your life. No one can decide if the person you are with is right, or wrong for you. If you should stay in your current relationship, or if you should leave. No one knows what is right for you in your life. Only you know those answers. YOU get to make those choices. We are all here in this world to grow and to travel down certain paths. Every circumstance and relationship you experience, you are meant to learn from, and grow within yourself. People are put in your life so you can work on who you are.

This became so true for me one day when I was being coached. My life coach said to me, "Christine, the reason for our relationships with other people, is for 'YOU' to do the work on 'yourself', and to learn how to be in control of how you react to their different behaviors." I had to question that for a minute. "What?" I asked her again to repeat that same sentence. So, she did, and then I questioned myself, thinking, "I don't think she knows exactly what she is talking about. Did she just say that relationships with other people are for me to do the work on myself? Really??? I think it may be time to move to Alaska. I won't have to deal with that many people then." Ugh, this work on oneself is so hard I thought. Then I was able to see that the bullshit that keeps coming up was not going to stop until I learned my lesson. And this has been pretty much my lesson all along, and I still fail at it from time to time. I know I need to learn these lessons to stop attracting them. One day I will succeed, I am sure of that. They don't happen as often as they used to. I am trying, I am working at it, and I will get there.

I AM STRONG, I AM POWERFUL, I AM A WOMAN.
Repeat that yourself.
I AM STRONG, I AM POWERFUL, I AM A WOMAN.

It's OK to Fail

It's OK to fail. It's OK to not have a win every time. When we fail it's an opportunity to learn from our mistakes. There may be times that we will repeat the same mistakes a few times before we catch onto them not working. Sometimes we never learn and stay in the cycle of repeat. We have all been there one time or another until we realized we were tired of not moving forward and staying stuck. Some of us stay stuck because we are afraid of change and then we never grow. Our brains tell us that change is uncomfortable and scary. Why would we want to change and grow when we are so comfortable by not having to move forward? Because the truth is whether or not you choose to move forward, you're going to get uncomfortable either way. If you choose to stay comfortable, by not failing, learning or growing, you are not going to stay happy because you will eventually get uncomfortable by not moving forward in life as we are meant to. We are meant to fail so we can grow and not continue repeating the same mistakes.

One day I decided I wanted to color my hair myself and it turned blue, silver, and a few other shades. I was going for silver. You know that really cool edgy silver. The edgy silver that some people are so fortunate to have as their natural hair. I was tired of being blonde for the past few years (let's be honest here, the bleach and the sun weren't really liking one another anymore, so they decided to call it quits and started frying my hair). I didn't have the patience to wait for an appointment, so I decided to become the expert colorist myself and mixed a few boxes of the edgy silver hair color that I ordered off of Amazon. Plus, I didn't want to blame my hairdresser if my hair came out horrible and I hated it. I was so excited; I was going to have the beautiful silver hair that the model on the box did (That is exactly what I envisioned). Yeah well that intention of mine that I set during meditation didn't work out how I planned that morning (you can't mess chemistry with universal beliefs, that shit just doesn't work). The color training that I took online by looking up the reviews didn't partake in my favor either.

I wound up turning my beautiful fried blonde hair to every shade of blue/green. OK, so I didn't read the instructions that said, if you have any gold tones in your hair, there is a possibility that your hair will turn blue or even green. Yikes. I am so blaming the print on the box for being so small that even with my reading glasses on I had absolutely no clue what the hell it said. Can someone tell me why the hell do they have to make the print so small ??? I mean don't they realize most people that are coloring their hair are older and need reading glasses? What the hell ??? So yes, I made a huge mistake and it's OK, because we all make mistakes. We all fail and it's OK. We are all human and we are still perfect no matter what hair color we have, mermaid colors and all.

You are perfect exactly how you are; it doesn't matter what others think. Other people's opinions about who you are or how you look don't matter—EVER!! I have to say, I wound up loving every minute of this mistake. I owned every bit of it. It was my failure and I loved myself for it. This is exactly how I felt when I started my own business as a Life Coach. Knowing that I would have to make mistakes, that I would have to fail over and over again if I ever wanted to get to my desired outcome.

You Are A Badass

It is normal that we all go through times when we feel overwhelmed for many different reasons. Trust me, I know those feelings don't feel good; I went through being uncomfortable almost every day when I started my new career. Doing all of the work on my own was fucking hard!!! There were days that I would sit there keeping myself distracted from what needed to get done. I didn't want to do the work, I didn't want to think about it, it was easier for me to just be on Instagram or Facebook liking everyone else's posts. I knew how hard it was to build a business from nothing. I didn't want to think about what I didn't know, having to learn it all, knowing that I was going to fail so many times. But I also knew if I didn't start taking massive action then I was not going to show up as the person that I want to be.

I knew I needed to show up for myself so I could help other people, I knew I wanted to help make a difference in women's lives. I knew what my calling was and I had to keep reminding myself that showing up is not only for me, it's for my clients. I wanted to help people learn to create their own happiness within themselves. I knew this when I signed up to become a Life Coach. I knew what I wanted, and I knew that for me to make that happen, I would have to already see myself there in my future. I am determined and I know the power that I have within myself. I will never let anything, or anyone stop me from creating the life I want to live... I am and will always be the creator of my dreams and no one will ever be able to take that from me.

You are a BADASS and you will always be able to create whatever you want. Don't let anything or anyone stop you from getting there and reaching your goals, whether it's a new house, a new career, a million dollars, a new relationship, a new car, to travel around the world, a second home, or financial freedom.

Pick your ass up off the couch and run towards it, like you're running for your life.

And DON'T STOP till you get there! Go after those dreams of yours. We vision them for a reason: to chase them and then create them. Life may not always be easy, but the hard work, and those uncomfortable days that you will go through, will get you to the other side of the rainbow. I promise.

It's your life and you can have whatever it is that you want, as long as you believe.

> *"I am not lucky. You know what I am? I am smart, I am talented. I take advantage of the opportunities that come my way and I work really, really, hard. Don't call me lucky. Call me a Badass."*
>
> **Shonda Rhimes**

Love the one you're with

Repeat after me:

I am a Powerful Badass and I will create the life I deserve.

Christinerizzo.com

About The Author

Christine is a Certified Life Coach, and probably a lot like you in many ways.

She absolutely loves her career because she gets to help women just like yourself, feel amazing by teaching them how they can have everything they have ever dreamed of.

Christine realized that she wanted to become a Life Coach when she was going through her divorce. She knew she always wanted to do something that would make a difference in other women's lives. Christine knew that she wanted to give back and serve other women by helping to empower them.

Christine works with women that were or that are still struggling in their marriage, relationships, or in their careers. Women who want to reinvent themselves or who don't feel confident with who they are in life. She helps women learn to love every bit of who they are so they can start feeling incredible, and start creating the happiness in their life that they deserve. She helps to empower women by teaching them how to take back their control.

Christine is truly thankful for her life and who she has become. If it wasn't for her experiences in her past, she wouldn't be the person she is today. She would not be the Coach she is today, helping all these amazing women learn to love exactly who they have always been all along.

If you would like to work with Christine, please visit her website at www.christinerizzo.com, or you can schedule a free 30 minute consultation with her at www.calendly.com/christinerizzocoaching

You can also follow her on her Instagram page @ Christinerizzo444, like her page on Facebook www.facebook.com/Christine.rizzodavi or follow her on her YouTube channel @ChristineRizzo

Acknowledgments

I want to thank my husband Frank for putting up with all my shit during the time it took to write this book. I would keep myself locked in my office and wouldn't come out for hours at a time. I also want to thank him for having to listen to the chapters of this book more than a dozen times and always making it like it was his first time ever hearing the words. I am grateful for his words of encouragement and the amount of support he has always given me for whatever I have always wanted to do. A huge thanks to my Spiritual Guide Daniel, I couldn't have created this book without him. He is the one that gave me the inspirational words during meditation, and in the middle of the night. I would wake up and either record what came to me or I would drag my ass out of bed and start typing away at 2 a.m. I want to thank my publishers over at Ultimate World Publishing, Nat and Stu Denman, Lendy Macario and Vivienne Mason, and my editor Marinda Wilkinson. If it weren't for them, this book would still be on my laptop, waiting to go to print. Most special of all, I wanted to thank YOU all for wanting to explore the power that you actually have within yourself, and to creating the life you deserve. You are the creator of your dreams and the creator of your reality. Remember, you are a powerful badass and you can have anything you want as long as you believe.

If you liked or loved this book, I would be so grateful if you left a review on Amazon, Barnes & Noble or wherever you purchased this book from. Thank you, Thank you, Thank you.

Notes

Christine Rizzo

Notes